Adolescent Brain 101

A Crash Course for Parents and Educators to Navigate Teen Mental Development, Emotional Well-being, and Academic Success

Joyce T.

Joyce T.

Copyright © 2024 by Joy & Co. Ventures LLC

All rights reserved.

This publication is designed to provide accurate and authoritative information in regard to the subject matter covered. It is sold with the understanding that neither the author nor the publisher is engaged in rendering legal, investment, accounting or other professional services. While the publisher and author have used their best efforts in preparing this book, they make no representations or warranties with respect to the accuracy or completeness of the contents of this book and specifically disclaim any implied warranties of merchantability or fitness for a particular purpose. No warranty may be created or extended by sales representatives or written sales materials. The advice and strategies contained herein may not be suitable for your situation. You should consult with a professional when appropriate. Neither the publisher nor the author shall be liable for any loss of profit or any other commercial damages, including but not limited to special, incidental, consequential, personal, or other damages.

Contents

Dedication

INTRODUCTION

"Adolescents are not monsters. They are just people trying to learn how to make it among the adults in the world, who are probably not so sure themselves." - Virginia Satir

This quote by Virginia Satir, a well-known family therapist, offers a refreshingly kind and honest perspective on adolescence. It reminds us that teenagers, who often get labeled as difficult, dramatic, or rebellious, aren't really trying to cause trouble. They're only doing their best to figure out how to exist in a world built by adults, many of whom, let's face it, are still trying to figure things out too.

What Satir does so beautifully here is challenge the tired old stereotypes. She shifts the narrative from judgment to empathy. Teens aren't fundamentally different from adults; they're just earlier in the process. They're working through new emotions, responsibilities, and expectations, all while trying to make sense of who they are and where they belong.

The quote levels the playing field a bit because truthfully, none of us has everything figured out. We're all navigating some form of uncertainty. When we acknowledge this, we create room for understanding and connection instead of conflict. We stop seeing adolescence as a problem to fix and start seeing it as a very human part of the journey.

The transition from childhood to adulthood is anything but straightforward. It's a winding, often messy journey filled with big shifts – not just in the body, but in the brain too. During adolescence, the brain goes through a dramatic transformation, laying the groundwork for adult thinking, emotions, and behavior.

But let's be honest: the very changes that help teens grow up can also make them incredibly impulsive. They may feel like nothing can touch them—like they're invincible. If you've ever found yourself exasperated saying something along the lines of, *"What can you do, she's a teenager!"* then you understand how things can get. This phrase captures the tension so many adults feel: loving someone who's growing fast but not always thinking things through.

Thankfully, our understanding of what's actually going on in the adolescent brain has come a long way. Thanks to tools like MRI (magnetic resonance imaging), researchers can now safely and non-invasively look inside the living brain – something that used to be impossible without serious risks. We're now able to see how different parts of the brain grow, connect, and communicate during the teen years, and this has provided real insight into why adolescence feels the way it does, for teens *and* for the people around them.

Understanding what's happening inside the teen brain can offer more than just scientific insight, though; it can help us better connect with the young people in our lives. That's what this book is all about: *understanding the teenage brain so we can move from just surviving these years to truly understanding and thriving through them.*

I'm not here just to rattle off brain science, I'm here as a fellow parent. I've asked the same questions you have, felt the same frustration, and celebrated those small, hard-earned victories. Together, we'll explore the wild range of teenage emotions, the impact of technology and social media, the pressures of academics, body image, peer dynamics, impulsivity, and everything in between.

It might feel overwhelming at times, but don't worry – I'll be with you at every step, helping to translate the science into real-life understanding. If you're ready to understand the mysteries of the adolescent brain and transform your relationship with the teens in your life, then let's dive in together. Consider yourself officially welcomed!

Chapter 1

The Teen Brain

What's Really Going On?

"We may not be able to prepare the future for our children, but we can at least prepare our children for the future."~Franklin D. Roosevelt

Adolescence is one of those life stages we tend to forget just how strange it felt when we were in it. Somehow, once we've made it through, we look at today's teens as if they're unpredictable aliens, forgetting we once felt just as misunderstood, confused, and emotionally intense.

But here's the thing: the teenage brain isn't broken, and teens aren't being dramatic for fun. Their brains are in the middle of a major renovation. And while it might seem like this all wraps up by the end of the teen years, the truth is that development continues well into the mid-twenties.

This chapter is about understanding what's really going on in a teen's brain when they're riding emotional roller coasters, glued to their screens, lashing out, sleeping until noon, bursting with creativity, or throwing themselves into causes bigger than themselves.

The Prefrontal Cortex

Let's start with the prefrontal cortex. This part of the brain acts like the boss, which simply means it is responsible for decision-making, impulse control, emotional regulation, planning, and long-term thinking.

But during the teen years, it is still pretty new to the job. It's learning how to lead, how to pause before reacting, and how to weigh consequences before making a call. So when your teen blurts something out or makes a snap decision that seems obviously unwise, it's not because they aren't thinking. It's because their brain's prefrontal cortex is still in training.

You might find yourself asking, "What were they thinking?" The answer? They *were* thinking, just not with a fully developed prefrontal cortex.

The Amygdala

Next, there's the amygdala—a small, almond-shaped part of the brain that acts like an emotional alarm system. It processes feelings like fear, anxiety, and anger. During adolescence, the amygdala is on high alert. It's hypersensitive, constantly scanning for threats, real or imagined.

That's why something small can feel like a full-blown crisis. I remember one evening when my son tore through the house in near panic because his hoodie had gone missing. To me, it seemed like a minor hiccup. But for him, it was huge. That wasn't "teen drama," it was his amygdala sounding the alarm.

For teens, the emotional volume is turned way up, while their reasoning system (the prefrontal cortex) is still catching up. That imbalance explains a lot.

Neuroplasticity

Now for the good news: the teenage brain is incredibly adaptable. Thanks to neuroplasticity – our brain's ability to rewire and grow – it's primed to learn, change, and develop new skills faster than at almost any other time in life.

Think of neuroplasticity as the brain's construction crew. Every time your teen tries something new, like learning guitar, coding, or speaking up in class, their brain is laying down fresh neural pathways.

My younger son, for instance, picked up coding last year. At first, it felt completely foreign to him. But with time and practice, I could almost see his brain wiring new connections – his once-baffled look was slowly replaced by a cool and collected confidence.

Putting It All Together

So, in a nutshell, during the teenage years, your kids' brain boss (prefrontal cortex) is learning the ropes, their emotion alarm (amygdala) is super-sensitive, and their brain's superpower (neuroplasticity) is making them into learning superheroes.

Here's the bottom line: when your teenager does something that makes you scratch your head, just take a deep breath. It's not chaos; it's their brain at work. With your understanding and guidance, their brain will keep growing and getting better at this adulting thing. And hey, we're all in this together!

On Brain Development

Let's take a step back and look at how the brain grows, from those squishy baby beginnings all the way to early adulthood. Understanding the big picture helps us appreciate just how much is happening inside our kids' heads, and why certain behaviors at different stages make so much more sense when we look beneath the surface.

Early Childhood

In the early years, a child's brain undergoes processes that are truly remarkable. Think of a toddler learning to walk – those unsteady steps, the constant falling and trying again, and then suddenly, one day, they're off and running. While this may seem like just a physical milestone, it is also brain wiring in action.

This phase is called **synaptogenesis**, where the brain is rapidly forming new connections. It's like laying down roads between different neighborhoods in the brain – millions of them. And just like any overbuilt system, it eventually needs a clean-up. That's where **synaptic pruning** comes in.

Imagine a gardener trimming a tree, cutting back the weak or unused branches so the strongest ones can thrive.

That's exactly what the brain does – it clears out what isn't being used to make room for stronger, faster, more efficient connections.

During this time, the brain is incredibly absorbent, like a super sponge. It soaks up everything – language, emotions, social cues, and routines. These early experiences become the blueprint for learning, behavior, and even long-term health. What a child is exposed to in these years *matters* more than we often realize.

Adolescence

Just when things feel like they've settled a bit, adolescence hits – and the brain launches into another huge phase of transformation. You could think of it as a second wave of construction, or like a massive software upgrade happening in real time.

Here, there's another round of synaptic pruning, this time focusing on higher-order thinking. The brain's efficiency is being fine-tuned, and **neuroplasticity** is at a high. This means teens are not only learning quickly, but also deeply affected by what they learn and experience during this stage.

But here's the catch: not all parts of the brain are developing at the same pace.

The amygdala, which handles emotions, fear, and rewards, matures earlier than the prefrontal cortex, the part responsible for impulse control, logic, and long-term planning. That's why teens can seem like walking contradictions – capable of deep insight one moment, and reckless decisions the next.

Add in the hormonal surges of puberty –testosterone, estrogen – and you've got what can feel like an emotional rollercoaster, complete with dramatic highs, confusing lows, and plenty of loop-the-loops.

Early Adulthood

As teens grow into young adults, the brain starts to stabilize. The prefrontal cortex finally catches up, and with that comes stronger decision-making, improved self-control, and more balanced emotional responses. The brain's boss—who's been in training all this time—finally steps into the role with confidence.

At this stage, the brain begins to lose some of its neuroplasticity, meaning it's not quite as quick to rewire as it was during adolescence. But the tradeoff is more consistency, more clarity, and a stronger sense of self.

And here's something powerful to remember: the habits, skills, and emotional patterns built during the teen years don't just fade away. They lay the groundwork for adult life. That's why these years are so important, not just for survival, but for shaping the future.

Besides the brain, hormones play a massive role in teen behavior. Let's see how.

Hormones and Teenagers

The Impact of Testosterone

Testosterone often gets a bad rap, but it's far more complex than we give it credit for. It works behind the scenes, shaping our teens' moods, energy, and tempo without stepping into the spotlight.

In boys, especially, testosterone levels surge during adolescence, sparking obvious physical changes like a deeper voice or facial hair. But it also impacts the brain, influencing their behavior in subtle and not-so-subtle ways. It can increase competitiveness, intensify drive, and fuel the desire to push limits.

This might look like your teen suddenly throwing themselves into extreme sports, heated debates, or ambitious social causes.

But testosterone isn't just about risk – it also plays a role in social bonding. It encourages loyalty, close friendships, and that fierce urge to stand up for their tribe.

Estrogen

Estrogen takes center stage during puberty for girls, directing the development of physical changes like breast development and menstruation. But just like testosterone, behind the scenes, it's doing so much more.

Estrogen has a strong influence on mood and emotion, often turning adolescence into an emotional rollercoaster. It interacts with the brain's serotonin system – our natural mood stabilizer – and helps regulate learning, memory, and emotional resilience.

So if your typically calm daughter suddenly bursts into tears over something small or seems overwhelmed for no obvious reason, it's not melodrama, it's biology. Estrogen is amplifying emotions and sensitivity, sometimes making things feel much bigger than they seem on the outside.

Cortisol

Cortisol is the body's built-in alarm bell. When teens experience stress (and let's face it, there's plenty of that in adolescence), cortisol kicks in to help them stay alert and focused. In the short term, it's actually helpful – like a natural energy boost before a test or performance.

But if stress is constant, cortisol sticks around too long, and that can take a toll. Chronic stress can dull the brain's pleasure response, pushing teens to chase bigger thrills just to feel good, whether that's taking risks, staying out too late, or diving deep into social media rabbit holes.

So the next time your teen does something impulsive or seems unusually reactive, try to pause before labeling it as rebellion.

Case Study

Unlocking the Teenage Brain through Neuroscience

We've touched a little on neuroscience, and in this section, we'll explore real-life scenarios that will put this into context. These are moments that might feel familiar if you're raising or working with teens. We'll also look at how popular films and TV shows reflect these challenges, offering insight into what teens are feeling, not just how they act.

These stories bring science to life, helping us understand not only what's happening *in* the brain, but also *because* of it.

The Impact of Stress on Decision-Making

Declan's Exam Meltdown

Declan, a high school student and my son's friend, had spent days preparing for a big math test. He did everything right – studied hard, practiced problems, even got help from his teacher. But on the morning of the exam, things fell apart. He overslept, skipped breakfast, and rushed to school in a panic. Despite all his prep, Declan told my son that he struggled, blanked on answers, second-guessed himself, and left the test feeling frustrated and defeated.

What the Brain Tells Us

Declan's experience isn't about laziness or lack of effort – it's biology working against him. The stress of the situation triggered a spike in cortisol, the body's primary stress hormone. And while a little cortisol can sharpen focus, too much of it interferes with brain function, especially in the prefrontal cortex, the part of the brain responsible for reasoning, memory, and decision-making.

In teens, this part of the brain is still developing, making it even more vulnerable to stress. So in Declan's case, the pressure didn't just rattle him – it hijacked his ability to think clearly in the moment.

Pop Culture Parallel: Euphoria

In *Euphoria*, we see this theme through Rue's character, who struggles under academic and emotional pressure, often turning to self-destructive habits. The show highlights how stress and the adolescent brain's fragility are deeply intertwined and how high the stakes can feel for teens trying to hold it all together.

Hormonal Influence on Mood Swings

Cassie's Emotional Whiplash

When Cassie, my friend's daughter, was 15, she used to be easygoing and upbeat. But then suddenly, everything seemed to set her off. She would cry over small misunderstandings, have sudden irritability, and an emotional intensity that left her parents confused and, quite frankly, worried.

What the Brain Tells Us

Cassie's emotional shifts are tied to the hormonal changes going on inside her body, particularly the role of estrogen, which surges during puberty. Estrogen doesn't just drive physical changes; it also interacts with serotonin, a neurotransmitter that regulates mood. When these systems are in flux, emotions can swing wildly – sometimes within the same afternoon.

So while Cassie's reactions seemed out of proportion, they were not made-up or attention-seeking; they were real. Her brain and body were simply adjusting to a new hormonal landscape, and as of writing this book, she's still is learning how to manage what she's feeling.

Pop Culture Parallel: The Fault in Our Stars

Hazel Grace, the main character in *The Fault in Our Stars*, captures this emotional depth beautifully. Her experiences show us just how layered and powerful teen emotions can be, especially when hormones, identity, and life's big questions collide.

The Role of the Prefrontal Cortex in Risk-Taking Behavior

Mike and His High-Flying Hobbies

Mike, 17, is the daredevil of my son's friend group. He's always chasing the next adrenaline rush—BMX tricks, cliff diving, skateboarding off rooftops. His parents watch with a mix of awe and terror, wondering why he seems drawn to danger.

What the Brain Tells Us

Mike's thrill-seeking isn't just a personality trait; it's brain development at work. As we said, during adolescence, the prefrontal cortex (the region that helps assess risks and long-term consequences) is still under construction. Meanwhile, the brain's reward system is firing on all cylinders, encouraging excitement, novelty, and sensation.

This mismatch, high motivation, and low impulse control, is a big reason why teens are more likely to take risks. For Mike, the promise of fun outweighs the thought of injury.

Pop Culture Parallel: Every Teen Adventure Flick Ever

From *Stranger Things* to *The Hunger Games*, we see teens risking everything, often without hesitation. These stories resonate not because they're unrealistic, but because they tap into something very real: the teenage brain's deep craving for challenge, meaning, and intensity.

However, it's crucial to recognize that each teenager is unique. Their experiences, temperament, and environment contribute to shaping their behavior. While neuroscience provides a general framework, it doesn't offer a one-size-fits-all explanation. But it can help you replace judgment with compassion.

So the next time you witness an emotional meltdown or a risky leap (literally or metaphorically), take a breath. There's more going on than meets the eye, and at least now, you know what that "more" really is.

Chapter 2

The Emotional Journey of Adolescence

A Closer Look At Emotional Development

"Adolescence is a new birth, for the higher and more completely human traits are now born." ~G. Stanley Hall

In this chapter, we'll see how teenagers begin to make sense of their feelings, how those feelings shape their behavior, and what this emotional journey means for the adults walking beside them. Let's start with emotional maturity first:

Understanding Emotional Maturity

Emotional maturity is a bit like learning to steer your own ship through unpredictable waters, but if you're a teenager, that ship is still being built while you're already out at sea. It's confusing, exhilarating, and at times overwhelming.

As the teenage brain develops, so does the ability to recognize and manage emotions. It doesn't happen all at once. At first, they learn to name what they're feeling, whether it's anger, joy, anxiety, or embarrassment. Then, with time and experience, teens begin to understand where those feelings come from and how to respond in ways that are healthy rather than reactive.

It's kind of like learning an instrument. At the beginning, it's just about hitting the right notes. But with practice, rhythm and expression start to emerge. Eventually, it becomes music: real, emotional, deeply personal music.

You can see this kind of growth in literature, too. Take *Harry Potter*, for instance. At the start of the series, Harry is just a boy trying to make sense of a confusing world. But as the story progresses, we watch him wrestle with grief, loyalty, anger, love, and loss—learning to respond with courage and heart. His emotional growth doesn't come from having all the answers, but from being willing to face hard truths and grow through them, just like teens in the real world.

The Role of Empathy in Emotional Development

Empathy, the ability to feel what someone else is going through, is one of the most powerful tools in a teenager's emotional toolbox. But it doesn't come automatically. It takes practice.

When teens begin to develop empathy, their relationships deepen. Friendships become more meaningful, conflicts start to make more sense and even family dynamics can shift, as teens begin to see their parents and siblings not just as people in their way, but as people with their own emotions and struggles.

A beautiful example of empathy in literature is found in *To Kill a Mockingbird*. Through her father, Atticus, young Scout Finch learns to see the world through others' eyes, even when it's hard. She begins to understand that people's actions often come from pain or fear, and that empathy can lead to compassion. Like Scout, teens begin developing empathy not all at once, but through real-life experiences, small lessons, and self-reflection.

Emotional Intelligence in Teens

Emotional intelligence—or EQ—is like a GPS for navigating the emotional terrain of adolescence. It includes self-awareness (knowing what you feel), self-regulation (managing how you express it), motivation, empathy, and social skills. When teens begin to strengthen these emotional muscles, they're better able to handle stress, connect with others, and bounce back from setbacks.

Think of it as a toolkit. It doesn't guarantee life will be easy, but it gives teens the tools to face hard moments with more calm, confidence, and perspective.

One of the most honest portrayals of emotional intelligence can be found in *The Perks of Being a Wallflower*. Through his letters, Charlie opens up about his confusion, pain, and search for connection. He doesn't always know what to do with his emotions, but he reflects on them with honesty and a hunger to understand. Over time, he learns how to sit with his feelings, talk about them, and reach out when he needs support. His journey is messy, but it's real. And it shows how powerful emotional intelligence can be, even when you're still figuring it all out.

The Powerful Role of Emotional Intelligence

When teens start to build emotional intelligence, they're not just preparing for high school or college; they're building a lifelong foundation. EQ helps them deal with disappointment, navigate conflict, find purpose, and build lasting relationships. And as adults, parents, teachers, and mentors, we play a key role in helping them develop these skills by modeling empathy, encouraging reflection, and staying present through the chaos.

A powerful example of emotional intelligence in context can be found in Frodo Baggins from *The Lord of the Rings*. Frodo's journey is filled with hardship, but what sets him apart isn't brute strength—it's his emotional strength. He shows resilience in the face of fear, compassion toward others in the fellowship, and an inner awareness that helps him resist the temptations of power. Frodo doesn't always get it right, but he leads with heart. And in many ways, that's what emotional intelligence is all about: not being perfect, but being human and choosing growth anyway.

How Do You Help Them Through Emotional Development?

Understanding aspects of emotional development in teenagers helps us guide them through this journey. As caretakers, we have the privilege of supporting them on this remarkable journey, offering guidance and understanding during these crucial years of emotional development.

Think about the classic coming-of-age novel *"The Catcher in the Rye"* by J.D. Salinger, where Holden Caulfield goes on a journey of self-discovery. Holden's caretakers, though not physically present, serve as guiding figures through his emotional turmoil. As readers, we witness the challenges of emotional development, the struggle to understand oneself, and the importance of supportive figures during this pivotal period.

This just goes to show you the essence of the role caretakers play in offering guidance and understanding during the crucial years of emotional development – and for your teen, you are the caretaker.

The Struggle of Emotional Regulation

Emotional Regulation Defined

Emotional regulation is quite a big concept, especially for teens. For them, it can feel a lot like trying to control the wind. Emotions come and go with such force and unpredictability, it's no wonder many of them feel overwhelmed by their inner world. But here's the hopeful part: like any skill, emotional regulation can be learned. With support, strategy, and practice, teens can begin to feel more in control of what they feel and how they respond.

In my own home, I've watched this unfold with my son, Mark. At first, managing emotions felt impossible for him. One moment he'd be calm, the next he'd be caught in a wave of frustration or sadness. But as we talked more openly about what was happening inside, and explored tools together, I began to see a shift. Emotional regulation wasn't some unreachable ideal—it was a muscle he could strengthen, one step at a time.

Identifying Emotional Triggers

We all have emotional triggers, those little buttons that, when pushed, set off big reactions. For teens, these can range from offhand comments about their appearance to the heavy weight of academic pressure. The first step in managing emotions is learning to recognize what sets them off.

With Mark, it became clear that school stress was one of his biggest triggers. We started noticing patterns: irritability before exams, withdrawal after tough assignments. I encouraged him to keep a simple feelings journal, just to write down what he was feeling and what happened right before. That tiny habit made a big difference. It helped both of us connect the dots, and it gave him a way to name what he was experiencing instead of just reacting to it.

This kind of self-awareness is the foundation of emotional regulation. When teens can anticipate what might set them off, they're far better equipped to manage how they respond.

The Role of Mindfulness

Mindfulness is a word that gets thrown around a lot these days, but at its core, it's really about being present, fully aware of what's happening in the moment without judgment. For teens, who often feel pulled in a million directions emotionally, mindfulness can be a lifeline.

We started with simple things. For Mark, just taking a few deep breaths before reacting to something stressful made a difference. It was like switching on a flashlight in a dark room. He began to notice his feelings more clearly before they took over, and over time, he started responding more thoughtfully.

Mindfulness doesn't have to be complicated. It can be a short breathing exercise, a walk where you focus on what you see and hear, or even just checking in with how your body feels. The goal isn't to eliminate feelings—it's to get curious about them instead of being ruled by them.

Guided Imagery

One of our favorite tools has been guided imagery. When things feel too intense or overwhelming, I'll gently ask Mark to close his eyes and picture a place that feels safe and calming, whether that's a forest, a beach, or even a cozy spot in our home. He takes a few minutes to imagine it in full detail: the sounds, the smells, the textures. It becomes his mental "reset button."

In those moments, it's like giving his brain a short vacation—a break from the noise and pressure. We also paired this with Progressive Muscle Relaxation, or PMR, another simple but powerful way to release built-up tension in the body.

Progressive Muscle Relaxation (PMR)

Stress often shows up in our bodies before we even realize what's wrong, for instance, tight shoulders, clenched jaws, or fidgety limbs. PMR helps teens tune into those physical signs of stress and learn how to let them go.

It works like this: you ask your teen to slowly tense and then relax each muscle group, starting from the feet and working their way up. With practice, it becomes almost automatic—a way to recognize when the body is holding stress and gently invite it to release.

Mark was skeptical at first (most teens are), but after a few sessions, he started requesting it on his own. It's now one of his go-to tools when he's feeling overwhelmed.

Keep in mind that no one masters emotional regulation overnight, least of all teens, whose brains and bodies are still learning how to handle the intensity of this life stage. But with patience, trust, and a few simple strategies, they can build the skills they need to ride out the emotional waves with more balance and confidence.

Managing Emotional Outbursts

Let's be honest, when it comes to teens, emotional outbursts are a consistent part of the ride. While they can be exhausting, they're also incredibly normal.

The key is not to fear the outbursts, but to help teens learn what to do afterward. Self-calming techniques like deep breathing can work wonders in the moment. When teens learn to slow their breath, they're actually turning off their brain's "fight-or-flight" switch, helping themselves calm down from the inside out.

With Mark, deep breathing became our go-to. In the early days, I'd remind him gently to pause and breathe. Now, he often catches himself and starts doing it without prompting. After the storm passes, we talk. We dig into what really caused the outburst: Was it frustration? Embarrassment? Pressure? That reflection has become a powerful part of his growth, turning difficult moments into learning ones.

Being a Role Model

It's easy to forget that our kids don't just listen to what we say, they watch what we do. When it comes to handling emotions, we are their blueprint.

I've made it a personal goal to be more intentional with how I express my own feelings. If I'm overwhelmed, I say it. If I need a moment, I take it. And when I mess up? I apologize. This models what healthy emotional regulation looks like.

Mark's picked up more than I realized. One day, after a rough evening, he said, "I need a minute to cool down—like you do." That's when I knew that our reactions as parents are indeed influential.

But remember, teaching emotional regulation isn't about never feeling upset. It's about showing our kids how to ride the wave without getting swept away.

Navigating the Emotional Sea

We've used the sea metaphor when it comes to teen emotions, so let's carry it along here as well. With adolescence, some days are calm, others stormy, and most have waves that come out of nowhere. Teens are learning basically how to sail, and our job, as parents or educators, is to be the compass they can turn to when the waters get rough.

We don't have to control the weather for them, but we can offer guidance, tools, and reassurance that they're not alone out there.

In our home, this metaphor has become part of our language. When Mark feels overwhelmed, I might say, "Looks like the waves are high today. Want help steering?" That simple shift—from reacting to guiding—has helped us both stay connected in the hard moments.

With time and practice, teens start to navigate their own emotions with more confidence. They become stronger, more self-aware, and more capable of sailing through whatever life throws at them.

The Impact of Stress on Teen Emotions

The Physiological Response to Stress

Imagine starting your morning with a sudden loud alarm, your heart races, your palms sweat, and you instantly feel alert. That's your body's stress response, and teens experience it all the time, not just in emergencies, but in everyday situations like tough tests, social pressure, or conflict with friends.

Their bodies release hormones like adrenaline and cortisol, preparing them to "fight or flee." But because their brains are still developing, that rush of stress can feel especially intense, and it can easily tip into frustration, anxiety, or even anger.

The Link Between Stress and Anxiety

Stress and anxiety are closely connected cousins. Stress often comes from a clear source, a deadline, a performance, or a confrontation. But anxiety can sneak up on you and stick around long after the stressor is gone. It's like the brain stays on high alert, even when there's no immediate danger.

When teens face chronic stress, their brains can get wired to expect the worst. For instance, a math test they did a while back that didn't go too well might trigger worry on a relaxing weekend. Their nervous system keeps ringing the alarm bell, even when the coast is clear.

I've seen this happen with Mark, especially around school. Even when things were going well, he'd feel unsettled—like something was about to go wrong. That's anxiety creeping in, whispering fear where calm should be.

Chronic Stress and Anxiety

Stress, in moderation, isn't all bad. It can motivate teens to study, perform, and grow. But when stress lingers—when it becomes a constant background hum—it can drain energy, disrupt sleep, and affect both physical and mental health.

That's why teaching teens how to *work with* stress is more important than trying to eliminate it. We can't protect them from every challenge, but we can give them tools to manage those challenges more effectively.

Start by helping them name what stress feels like in their bodies. Do they get headaches? Feel tense? Lose focus? That kind of awareness is the first step in self-regulation.

Navigating the Sea of Stress

Stress can feel overwhelming, but with the right tools—and the right support—teens can learn to ride those waves, even appreciate them as part of their growth.

Our role isn't to remove all stress, but to help teens become resilient. That means teaching them to breathe, to reflect, to rest when they need it, and to reach out when it gets too much.

In our family, we talk about stress the same way we talk about the weather. Some days are stormy. Some are bright. But every day is navigable with the right map and mindset.

Let's keep helping them cope and reminding them that we're right there, sailing beside them.

Case Studies

Handling Emotional Outbursts Explained

In this section, we will cover several real-life examples and what to do, just in case you find yourself in similar situations:

Scenario 1: Dealing with Academic Pressure

Explanation:

Laura's emotional outbursts are triggered by the stress of upcoming finals. In this scenario, providing support involves a multifaceted approach:

Validating Emotions:

Why: Emotional validation helps Laura feel understood and acknowledged.

How: Encouraging her to express her feelings and reassuring her that stress is a normal response to academic challenges.

Study Strategies:

Why: Breaking down tasks reduces anxiety and makes studying more manageable.

How: Assisting Laura in creating a study schedule, allowing her to focus on one task at a time, promoting a sense of control.

Prioritize Self-Care:

Why: Self-care enhances mood and cognitive function, crucial during stressful times.

How: Reminding Laura to maintain regular meals, engage in physical activity, and get adequate sleep.

Perspective on Grades:

Why: Reinforcing that worth is not solely defined by grades promotes a healthier mindset.

How: Offering reassurance, highlighting strengths, and acknowledging achievements outside academics.

Scenario 2: Managing Family Conflict

Explanation:

Lily's emotional outbursts stem from frequent conflicts with her parents. Addressing this situation involves building healthy communication and conflict resolution skills:

Open Communication:

Why: Creating an open and respectful family environment fosters understanding.

How: Encouraging active listening and providing a platform for family members to express feelings and perspectives.

Expressing Feelings:

Why: Teaching Lily to express feelings calmly reduces confrontations.

How: Introducing the use of "I" statements to communicate personal feelings without blaming or criticizing.

Empathy:

Why: Empathy promotes understanding, reducing conflict.

How: Emphasizing the importance of seeing situations from different perspectives, cultivating a more empathetic family dynamic.

Emotional outbursts during adolescence are a common aspect of emotional development. The most important thing is to understand the causes behind such outbursts, acknowledge emotions, and equip teenagers with strategies to express feelings healthily.

Chapter 3

The 3 Factors

The Persistent Triad in Teen Development

"Even as kids reach adolescence, they need more than ever for us to watch over them. Adolescence is not about letting go. It's about hanging on during a very bumpy ride." ~Ron Taffel

There always seem to be a few pieces of the puzzle that show up again and again when it comes to teens, and they're not always easy to figure out. But if you look closely, three key factors stand out as powerful forces that shape nearly every teen's experience.

In this chapter, we'll take a look at those three core influences, beginning with one that's often underestimated but deeply important: sleep.

The Late-Night Mystery Explained

Changes in Sleep Cycle

Teens are notorious night owls – we all know it. But what's really going on under the surface? Is it that they force themselves awake, or are there biological factors at play that keep them awake?

Sleep Phase Delay

The body's internal clock, known as the circadian rhythm, experiences a shift called sleep phase delay during adolescence. This leads to increased alertness later in the evening, making early bedtimes challenging. This biological shift helps you understand why teens may naturally struggle with early bedtimes.

Morning Wake-Up

The natural tendency for teens to wake up later is a result of their set internal clock. Recognizing this biological aspect can help you to reframe possible perceptions of your teen(s) being lazy and emphasize the importance of aligning schedules with their natural sleep patterns.

Impact on Health and Academics

Health Effects

Poor sleep during adolescence can affect mood, energy levels, and physical health, which adds stress to the already existing emotional rollercoaster of adolescence. This highlights the interconnectedness of sleep and overall well-being during a crucial developmental period.

Academic Performance

You've probably seen it: your teen staying up late to cram for a test, hoping those last-minute study hours will give them an edge. But here's the truth, without enough sleep, the brain struggles to absorb, process, and hold on to new information. Those late-night efforts might actually backfire. Helping teens connect the dots between sleep and academic success reinforces the message that rest isn't a luxury; it's part of the plan.

Tips for Healthy Sleep Habits

Consistent Schedule

Encourage a consistent sleep schedule, even on weekends. This is recommended to help your teen align with the internal clock. Consistency is a key factor in making sure this is possible.

Bedroom Environment

The bedroom should be a place of calm. Encourage teens to create a quiet, cozy environment that supports good sleep. Things like blackout curtains, earplugs, or a soft white noise machine can help. Even little changes in lighting or temperature can make a big difference.

Limit Screen Time

Phones, tablets, and TVs give off blue light that messes with melatonin, the hormone that helps us sleep. Powering down screens at least an hour before bed can help teens wind down naturally. This might be the hardest habit to change, but it's also one of the most effective.

Get Moving

Daily exercise, especially in the morning or early afternoon, helps teens sleep better at night. Physical activity boosts the body's natural rhythms and can reduce anxiety and restlessness, two major sleep disruptors.

<u>Wind Down Routine</u>

Bedtime routines aren't just for toddlers. Teens benefit from relaxing rituals too, whether it's reading a book, taking a warm shower, or doing a few minutes of mindful breathing. These small habits signal the brain that it's time to shift from busy mode to rest mode.

Now, let's move on to the second factor:

Rebellion

The Rebellious Stage as a Quest for Independence

In homes worldwide, the familiar scene of a defiant teenager breaking rules plays out. However, beyond this stubbornness lies the deep need for autonomy and independence, which, if we may resist, we may view as rebellion.

Let's understand this in detail:

Drive for Autonomy

- Powerful Urge: The teenage drive for autonomy is a deep-seated urge to control their lives, not mere rebellion.

- Becoming Independent: Teens want to make choices, learn from mistakes, and carve their own path. It's a healthy step toward independence.

Role of Peer Influence

- Peer Power: Peers wield influence during adolescence, both positive and negative, amplifying the drive for independence.

- Positive Influence: Peers can inspire positive independence, encouraging teens to explore, try new activities, and find a sense of belonging.

Ways to Support Healthy Independence

- Negotiate Boundaries: Involve your teens in setting boundaries through discussion, fostering autonomy, and teaching negotiation skills.

- Encourage Decision-Making: Provide opportunities for them to make decisions, which can boost their confidence and refine decision-making skills.

- Respect Privacy: Respect their need for physical and emotional privacy to build trust and reinforce autonomy.

- Support Interests: Encourage them to explore their interests and hobbies, providing avenues for self-expression and independence.

- Guide, Don't Control: Remember to focus on guiding rather than controlling. Share wisdom, provide advice, and let them make decisions, fostering autonomy while assuring support.

Real-Life Scenario

Susan and Ben

Susan was a single mother to her son Ben and their home had started to feel like a battleground. Ben was pushing back on rules, staying out late, and constantly questioning everything Susan asked of him. At first, it felt like rebellion, like he was deliberately testing her boundaries just to make life harder.

But over time, Susan began to shift her approach. Instead of reacting with frustration, she started to really listen. She realized that Ben's behavior wasn't about disrespect, it was his way of asserting independence, of saying, "I need to figure out who I am."

Through open conversations, Susan made space for Ben to express himself. They talked about why certain rules mattered and where there could be room for flexibility. As time went by, it became clear that Ben wasn't trying to push her away; he was trying to find his own footing in the world.

Rebellion, as it turns out, is often less about defying authority and more about discovering identity. When we approach it with patience, curiosity, and respect, it becomes a chance to strengthen, not sever, the connection with our teens.

Now, on to the third factor:

The Social Aspect

Teens and Their Tribal Tendencies

As kids move into adolescence, peers often take center stage where they once looked to parents for approval. This is a natural, necessary part of growing up. Teens are wired to seek connection outside the home as they begin carving out their own identity.

In this section, we will see why peer relationships matter so much during this stage, how social dynamics shape behavior, and what we can do to support teens as they navigate their "tribe."

Importance of Peer Relationships

Shift in Spotlight

- Explanation: Adolescence redirects attention from family to friends, emphasizing the increasing influence of peer opinions.

- Relevance: Recognizing this shift helps parents and caregivers understand the evolving dynamics in teens' lives.

Emotional Support

- Explanation: Peer relationships serve as a safe space for teens to share emotions, fostering a sense of belonging and understanding.

- Relevance: Highlighting the emotional support aspect underscores the importance of these relationships in teens' lives.

Role of Social Acceptance

Guiding Rhythm

- Explanation: Acceptance by peers is portrayed as the guiding rhythm in teenage social life, aligning with the human need for social connection.

- Relevance: Understanding the importance of social acceptance helps caregivers navigate and support teens in their social interactions.

Validation and Self-Esteem

- Explanation: Social acceptance is linked to the validation of teens' self-worth, contributing to boosted self-esteem and reinforced identity.

- Relevance: Connecting social acceptance to self-esteem highlights its profound impact on teens' mental and emotional well-being.

Conformity Pressures

- Explanation: The pursuit of acceptance can lead to conformity, influencing attitudes, behaviors, and choices to fit in.

- Relevance: Acknowledging conformity pressures raises awareness of the challenges teens may face in balancing their individuality with the desire for acceptance.

In the next chapter, we turn our attention to something often felt but not always seen – the emotional and mental health struggles that many teens quietly carry. Behind the eye rolls, mood swings, or silence at dinner, there can be deeper challenges like anxiety, stress, or even depression.

Let's understand this better.

Chapter 4
The Teen Brain and Mental Health
Unmasking the Invisible Battles

"We live in a world where mental health is real. Emotional health is real, and people feel like no one cares."- Malik Yoba

We've spent some time exploring the teen brain, how it develops, what influences it, and how emotions and peer dynamics come into play. But now, we're zooming in on something just as critical, yet often hidden beneath the surface: mental health.

Let's be honest, teenage life is a lot. Between navigating friendships, growing independence, academic stress, and figuring out who they are, teens are often juggling more than we realize. On the outside, everything might seem fine, like that laid-back kid at a party who looks totally chill. But underneath, there might be a mental and emotional tug-of-war going on.

At the core of it is the developing teen brain. While we've already explored how the prefrontal cortex is still maturing and the limbic system often takes the lead, here's where it becomes more than just a quirky phase. This mismatch between emotional highs and a still-learning logic system can make teens more vulnerable to anxiety, depression, and emotional overwhelm. And often, those feelings aren't voiced – they're masked.

This chapter is about unmasking it all. It's about understanding how mental health challenges show up during adolescence—not always loudly, but deeply. We'll explore what's really going on inside, why some teens are more vulnerable than others, and how we as parents, caregivers, and educators can spot the signs and offer meaningful support.

Indeed, there's no magic fix, but there is power in empathy, awareness, and early action. As we dig deeper, we will not only learn about the adolescent mind but also how to walk beside our teens with compassion and an understanding presence, which is what they need from us.

We will do this through quick descriptions that you can easily understand.

Let's go!

Navigating Anxiety and Stress in the Teen Maze

Recognizing Signs of Anxiety

- Description: Anxiety is a master of disguise, wearing different masks such as restlessness, physical discomfort, and avoidance behaviors.

- Example: Your teenager might steer clear of social situations, express physical symptoms like a racing heart, or undergo changes in sleep and eating patterns.

Impact on Daily Life

- Description: Anxiety acts as a lens distorting a teenager's view of the world, affecting various aspects of their daily life, including school, social interactions, hobbies, and family time.

- Example: Within the classroom, anxiety may

create challenges in concentration and active participation, turning routine tasks into daunting sources of stress.

Strategies for Stress Management

<u>Open Conversations:</u>

- Description: Create a safe and non-judgmental space for your teenager to openly express fears and worries.

- Example: Employ empathetic responses such as *"That sounds really tough"* to foster an environment conducive to open dialogue.

<u>Breathing Exercises</u>

- Description: Introduce simple yet effective techniques like deep breathing to help calm the nervous system.

- Example: Encourage the regular practice of these exercises as a proactive measure whenever anxiety starts to surface.

Mindfulness Practices

- Description: Incorporate mindfulness practices, such as meditation or yoga, to keep teens grounded in the present moment.

- Example: Suggest the integration of mindfulness techniques into their daily routine as a tool for managing stress.

Encourage Physical Activity

- Description: Promote regular physical exercise as a healthy outlet for anxiety, leveraging the mood-boosting effects of endorphins.

- Example: Encourage participation in sports, dance, or other fitness activities as part of their routine.

Balanced Diet and Sleep

- Description: Emphasize the crucial role of nutrition and adequate sleep in regulating mood and stress levels.

- Example: Discuss the connection between a

well-balanced diet, quality sleep, and overall emotional well-being.

Seek Professional Help

- Description: Recognize the severity of anxiety when it significantly interferes with daily life and advocate for the involvement of mental health professionals.

- Example: Take proactive steps to connect your teenager with a supportive therapist or counselor who specializes in adolescent mental health.

Depression in Teens

Recognizing Signs of Teen Depression

Teen depression often sneaks in quietly, disguising itself as typical teenage behavior. For instance, Jane, a close friend's daughter, started becoming more irritable, reacting strongly to minor annoyances. She withdrew into solitude, spending long hours alone in her room. Jane's parents noticed that the activities she once enjoyed, like playing the guitar or painting, lost their luster, replaced by a pervasive indifference.

As depression took hold of Jane, her academic performance started to falter. Her once-enthusiastic participation in school clubs and sports became an afterthought, and meals went untouched. Constant fatigue plagued her, like a car running on empty.

Also, Jane's sleep patterns shifted, with nights spent staring at the ceiling and days lost to excessive sleep.

The Crucial Role of Support and Understanding

In the face of teen depression, your role as a parent or educator becomes crucial. If you notice signs of depression in your teen, approach them with kindness and empathy. For instance, Tom, a neighbor's son. Tom's parents initiated a conversation, not a confrontation. They let him know they had noticed his struggle and that they were there to help, free from judgment or criticism.

Tom's parents utilized active listening techniques to convey genuine interest. They allowed him to express his feelings, fears, and struggles without interruption or the pressure of quick fixes. Their mere presence and understanding proved immensely helpful to Tom. Even if you can't fully grasp their experience, acknowledge their pain and validate their feelings.

For example, when Tom expressed feelings of worthlessness or guilt, his parents reassured him that it's okay to feel the way he does and reminded him that he's not alone. They communicated that depression is treatable, and with the right help, he can overcome it.

The Importance of Professional Help

While your support is invaluable, professional help often becomes necessary in dealing with teen depression. Take Jess, a family friend's daughter, for instance. A mental health professional provided a safe space for her to explore her feelings and equipped her with effective coping strategies.

Psychotherapy, especially cognitive-behavioral therapy (CBT) and interpersonal therapy (IPT), proved effective in treating Jess's teen depression. In some cases, medication was recommended, helping to balance brain chemicals and alleviate symptoms. Jess's parents emphasized that seeking professional help is not a sign of weakness but a step towards healing.

They reminded her that taking care of mental health is as important as physical health. Jess, like many others, needed to be reassured that she is not alone, help is available, and things can get better.

Navigating the Storm towards Hope and Healing

Depression can feel like a heavy storm cloud settling over what should be a bright, spirited season of life. For many teenagers, it quietly creeps in, sometimes showing up as sadness, sometimes as anger, withdrawal, or simply exhaustion. And for the adults who love them, it can be confusing and painful to witness.

But here's the hopeful part: depression is not the end of the road. With compassion, understanding, and the right support—whether through family, school, therapy, or all of the above—healing is not only possible, it's within reach.

Understanding Academic Stress and the Teen Brain

The Shadow of Academic Stress

In the middle of the highs and lows of adolescence, one factor stands tall like a towering skyscraper: academic stress. It rises above everything with school deadlines, tough exams, never-ending homework, college applications, and the unspoken pressure to always do more, be more, achieve more.

This pressure doesn't come from one place. It builds slowly, from expectations at home, comparisons with peers, the pursuit of perfection, and sometimes, from teens' own inner critics. The message they receive again and again is clear: their worth is tied to their grades, their test scores, and their accomplishments. But where does that leave space for their creativity, their kindness, their joy?

The Balancing Act

It's true that a little pressure can be motivating. It can spark ambition and help teens discover what they're capable of. But when that pressure becomes constant, when the fear of failure overshadows the love of learning, it turns something potentially positive into a chronic source of stress. Suddenly, the drive to do well becomes a burden teens carry every day.

The Complex Relationship with Mental Health

Academic stress doesn't exist in a vacuum. It's deeply ingrained into a teenager's life and emotions, test by test, grade by grade. When the pressure starts to build, it doesn't just affect how they perform in school; it affects how they see themselves.

Over time, constant stress can wear down even the most resilient teen. It can quietly open the door to anxiety, self-doubt, or depression. And because the teenage brain is still developing—particularly the areas that regulate emotion—teens often don't yet have the tools to manage that pressure in a healthy way.

What's more, when academic achievement becomes the measuring stick for worth, a single low grade can feel like a personal failure. Instead of seeing it as just a rough day or a tough subject, they may internalize it: *"I'm not smart enough," "I'll never catch up,"* or even, *"I'm a disappointment."* Their self-esteem starts to ride the highs and lows of their report cards, turning school into something that brings them great stress.

Strategies for a Balanced Academic Life

Think of academic pressure like steam building in a pressure cooker; it can be useful in small amounts, but if there's no way to release it, things can explode. That's why it's so important to help teens find their own "release valves,"small, sustainable ways to manage stress before it becomes overwhelming:

Prioritize and Plan

Teach your teen to prioritize tasks based on urgency and importance. Using planners or digital tools to organize tasks and deadlines can help manage workload effectively and reduce stress.

Break it Down

Encourage your teen to break large tasks or projects into smaller, manageable parts. This approach makes the overall task seem less overwhelming and more achievable.

Healthy Study Habits

Promote healthy study habits, including regular breaks, studying in a quiet environment, and avoiding last-minute cramming. Effective study techniques like active recall and spaced repetition can enhance learning.

Self-Care

Remind your teen of the importance of self-care, encompassing regular exercise, a balanced diet, and adequate sleep. These practices can boost mood, energy levels, and cognitive function, contributing to effective stress management.

Open Communication

Maintain open lines of communication with your teen. Let them know they can share academic concerns without fear of judgment or criticism. Validate their feelings and stressors, reassuring them of your unconditional support.

In the face of academic stress, it's crucial to remind teenagers that their academic achievements do not define their worth. They are more than a score on a test or a grade on a report card; they are individuals bursting with potential, each possessing unique strengths, passions, and dreams.

Nurturing Resilience and Individuality

As parents and educators, our role is to help navigate academic stress, providing the tools needed to create a balanced academic life. We support, understand, and stand by our teenagers, showing them they are not alone in their struggles. We emphasize the importance of mental health and celebrate their individuality, valuing who they are over what they achieve on a test.

In the next part of this chapter, we'll take a closer look at something every teenager needs in their emotional toolkit: resilience. It's one of the most important qualities we can help them build. We'll explore what resilience really means, why it matters so much in adolescence, and how the relationships in a teen's life—especially with family, teachers, and friends—play a powerful role in shaping it.

Crafting Emotional Armor for Teens

The Power of Resilience

If there's one quality that carries teens through the ups and downs of growing up, it's resilience. Think of it like a strong, flexible sailboat—able to stay afloat and steer even when the winds shift and the waves get rough. It doesn't mean the storm won't come. It just means your teen has what it takes to make it through—and even come out stronger.

Resilience isn't about avoiding problems or always staying calm under pressure. It's about learning how to recover when things go wrong, how to keep going even when the path isn't clear, and how to believe in yourself even when you're shaken. When stress, anxiety, or setbacks show up (as they often do), resilience gives teens the confidence to keep moving forward—to ask for help when they need it, to face fears with courage, and to know deep down: "I can get through this."

The Crucial Role of Positive Relationships

Resilience is a connection that is nurtured – with parents, siblings, teachers, friends, and mentors. These relationships form the scaffolding that supports teens as they learn to weather life's challenges.

- **Parents**

Your steady presence is more powerful than you might think. When your teen knows you're there no matter what, with love that doesn't waver and support that doesn't depend on performance, they feel grounded. That deep sense of being seen and accepted gives them the confidence to face hard things and the self-worth to bounce back after failure.

- **Teachers**

A kind, supportive teacher can make all the difference. In a safe, inclusive classroom where students are encouraged to try, fail, and try again, teens begin to see mistakes not as dead ends but as part of the process. When teachers believe in them—even on the days they struggle—it plants the seed of resilience.

- **Friends and Mentors**

Peers and trusted adults outside the family also play a big role. In the messiness of adolescence, having someone to laugh with, vent to, or share life's weird little moments with helps teens feel understood and less alone. Through these shared experiences, they learn about mutual support, empathy, and standing by others through thick and thin.

Strategies for Building Resilience

Here are some thoughtful, practical ways to support your teen in developing the emotional grit they need for the road ahead:

Promote Problem-Solving Skills

When your teen is facing a tough situation, resist the urge to jump in with the answer. Instead, sit beside them and work through it together. Help them see the issue not as an impossible wall but as a puzzle that can be figured out step by step. Brainstorm ideas, weigh the pros and cons of each option, and guide them toward choosing their own path forward. You're not just solving one problem—you're teaching them how to face many.

Foster a Growth Mindset

Cultivate a growth mindset in your teen. Teach them that abilities and intelligence can be developed with effort and persistence. Emphasize the value of hard work, perseverance, and grit in achieving their goals.

Encourage Self-Expression

Provide ample opportunities for your teen to express their feelings, thoughts, and ideas. Whether through conversations, journal writing, or creative activities like art and music, self-expression boosts self-esteem and fosters a sense of control, both crucial for resilience.

Nurture Optimism

Life won't always be easy, but helping your teen learn to spot the silver lining can make a world of difference. Talk with them about challenges as temporary rather than permanent. Encourage them to notice what went right, even in hard situations. By no means is optimism about denying pain; it's about believing there's still a way forward.

Validate Feelings

Validate your teen's feelings. Acknowledge their emotions without judgment or criticism. Let them know it's okay to feel upset, scared, or sad, as validation enhances emotional awareness and regulation.

As parents and educators, resilience is one of the greatest gifts we can give our teens. Every moment we spend guiding them, listening to them, and walking beside them through setbacks is like adding another plank to the ship they'll eventually sail on their own. And with every storm they weather, they grow sturdier, braver, and more sure of who they are.

Next, we'll turn our focus to another major force shaping the teen experience today: **technology and social media**. How is it affecting their attention, self-image, and mental health? How do we help them find balance in a world that never turns off? Let's see this together in the next chapter.

Chapter 5
THE DIGITAL DILEMMA

Navigating the Impact of Technology on the Adolescent Brain

"As the world becomes a more digital place, we cannot forget about the human connection".
-Adam Neumann

We're raising kids in a world that's changing at lightning speed, especially when it comes to technology. From smartphones to social media, today's teens are growing up with digital tools that we, as adults, never had to navigate during our own adolescence. And while there's no doubt that these tools have transformed how we communicate, connect, and learn, they're also shaping something far more intimate and delicate: the teenage brain.

A recent study published in *JAMA Pediatrics* shed new light on this digital-age phenomenon. The findings suggest that frequent social media use may be doing more than keeping teens glued to their phones—it could actually be influencing the way their brains develop. Specifically, the study found that habitual use appears to activate brain regions linked to **social rewards and punishments**, nudging young brains to become more sensitive to peer feedback.

What's Really Going On in the Brain?

Researchers observed that adolescents who regularly check social media show changes in areas of the brain tied to emotion and decision-making, especially the amygdala (as we saw, our emotional radar) and the dorsolateral prefrontal cortex (the part responsible for reasoning and judgment). These regions seem to be tuning themselves to seek social rewards, likes, comments, views, and avoid perceived social rejection.

It's important to pause here: this doesn't necessarily mean that social media is harming their brains. But it does point to an important shift. These teens may be developing heightened sensitivity to social cues, both online and off, which could shape how they engage with the world around them.

Because adolescence is such a crucial time for brain development, the big question is: What does this mean long-term? That's still unclear. The science is still catching up. But what we do know is this: the brain is adaptable. Thanks to the concept of neuroplasticity, which we covered earlier, the brain can rewire itself based on experiences, meaning these changes are not necessarily permanent.

Screen Time and Childhood Development

And it's not just teens. This research adds to a broader conversation about screen time and its effects on younger children, especially during early development. For instance, excessive screen exposure in toddlers has been linked to language delays and attention challenges.

Then came the pandemic—a time when screens became lifelines for school, socializing, and sanity. But the dramatic increase in screen time during this period created new complexities. Virtual learning, Zoom fatigue, isolation from peers, etc., these experiences have left lasting imprints, and we're still working to fully understand them.

Your Role as a Parent

One thing we do know is that parents play a crucial role in helping teens navigate their digital world. And since the prefrontal cortex is still under construction until around age 21, teenagers often need someone to step in as a kind of temporary stand-in.

Think of yourself as a "surrogate frontal lobe." You're there to help them pause, reflect, weigh consequences, and learn how to make better decisions online and offline.

This doesn't mean taking control or banning all screen time. It means creating open, ongoing conversations about what they're seeing, feeling, and experiencing online. It means talking about both the good and the bad—how social media can connect us but also leave us feeling left out or judged.

It's easy to slip into an all-or-nothing mindset when it comes to tech, either it's ruining our kids, or it's the greatest innovation ever. But the truth is somewhere in between. Social media and screen time can be both empowering and overwhelming. Teens can use digital platforms to explore their passions, connect with others, and find their voice. But they also need guidance to recognize when their use becomes excessive or starts to impact their well-being.

That's where you come in—as the steady, compassionate voice reminding them of their worth beyond likes and shares, and helping them find balance in a digital world that never really powers down.

In this chapter, we'll explore the delicate relationship between technology—particularly social media—and the adolescent brain. As our world becomes increasingly digital, screens have become a central part of daily life, especially for teens. Social media, in particular, plays a powerful role in how they communicate, connect, and view themselves.

We'll dive into what current research is revealing about how frequent use of social media might be influencing brain development, especially in areas linked to emotions, judgment, and sensitivity to social feedback. While some of these findings raise important questions, they also offer insight into how adaptable and responsive the teenage brain truly is.

Let's get started:

Navigating the Digital Landscape

In this constantly buzzing digital world, teens often find themselves doing five things at once: texting a friend, scrolling through Instagram, watching YouTube, flipping between homework tabs, and maybe even listening to music in the background. It feels like multitasking, and on the surface, it might even seem productive.

But here's the truth: the brain doesn't work that way. Research tells us that this kind of multitasking actually drains mental resources. It's like trying to listen to three different radio stations at the same time—you don't really catch the full message from any of them. Instead of saving time, multitasking often leads to more mistakes, lower productivity, and mental fatigue.

And the impact doesn't stop there. All that screen time—especially at night—can wreak havoc on sleep. The blue light from devices messes with melatonin, the hormone that helps us fall asleep. Think of it like having a digital espresso shot right before bed. Add in how engaging and addictive digital content can be, and suddenly it's midnight before your teen even notices the time. Over time, this lack of rest chips away at mood, focus, and overall well-being.

So, how do we help our teens navigate this fast-paced digital terrain without completely cutting them off from the world they live in?

To do this, here are some guidelines:

Set Clear Boundaries

Establish a family media plan with clear boundaries for screen time. Rules such as no screens during meals or a digital curfew an hour before bed can be effective. It's crucial to lead by example, as actions speak louder than words.

Encourage Mindful Usage

Teach teens to use technology mindfully. They should pay attention to the time spent on different activities and how those activities make them feel. Just as a balanced food diet is about conscious choices, a digital diet seeks equilibrium.

Promote Offline Activities

Advocate for a balance between screen time and offline activities like physical exercise, reading, hobbies, or time spent in nature. It's akin to enriching a diet with a variety of nutrients.

<u>Use Parental Control Tools</u>

Consider parental control tools to monitor and limit screen time. These tools should be a last resort, used with your teen's knowledge and consent. The aim is to guide, not police, their digital interactions.

Managing screen time isn't about demonizing technology but helping teenagers use it to enhance their lives. The goal is for them to navigate this world with confidence and ease, reaping the benefits while mitigating the risks.

Balancing Offline and Online Lives

It's easy for teens to get swept up in the digital current: scrolling through social media, binge-watching videos, gaming, or staying constantly connected through messaging apps. But while technology is an unavoidable part of their lives, it's important to remind them (and ourselves) that life doesn't only happen on a screen.

This balance is crucial. While the digital world offers connection, entertainment, and even learning, it's just one part of the whole. The offline world, such as cooking a new recipe, painting just for fun, journaling, playing an instrument, brings depth. These moments foster confidence, self-expression, and the kind of joy that doesn't depend on likes or shares.

Even quiet, seemingly unproductive things like daydreaming, kicking a ball around, or lying in the grass watching clouds have their place. They give teens the mental space they don't always realize they need. In a world that's always on, the value of slowing down can't be overstated.

Implementing a Digital Detox: Practical Approaches

Helping your teenager take a break from screens doesn't have to feel like starting a war. With the right approach, it can be a gentle shift toward healthier habits.

Here are some practical tips to support a more balanced relationship with technology:

Schedule Tech-Free Time

Designate specific periods each week as tech-free, for example, during meals, an hour before bedtime, or an unplugged day over the weekend.

Encourage Engaging Offline Pursuits

Inspire your teenager to take part in offline activities they enjoy, such as arts and crafts, sports, music, or cooking. Assist them in discovering activities that bring both joy and fulfillment.

Set a Positive Example

Demonstrate positive digital usage habits. Let your teenager observe you reading a book, gardening, or pursuing a hobby, to set a solid example of the value and enjoyment of offline activities.

Establish a Tech-Free Zone

Create designated tech-free zones in your home, be it the dining table, the living room, or a cozy reading nook.

As your teen works on striking this balance, they'll gradually learn that life isn't about the number of likes on a post or the high score in a video game. It's about the simple joys and life, in all its beauty, should be experienced both online and offline.

Chapter 6

Effective Communication with Your Teen

An Art Worth Mastering

"There's one thing you can start doing right now that will change how you communicate with any young human: Remember what it's like to be one." —— Justin Young

There's one incredibly simple yet powerful switch you can flip, and it has the potential to completely transform the way you connect with the younger generation. This is all about taking a stroll down memory lane, back to the days when you were experiencing the twists and turns of adolescence. Yes, this is the secret sauce—rekindling that empathy by tapping into your own past.

I mean, let's be real. Remembering what it's like to be a young human isn't just a trip down nostalgia lane; it's a game-changer in how you communicate and relate to your teen. That's what Justin Young captures so perfectly in the quote above. When we take the time to reflect on our own teenage years, we don't just become better listeners—we become more understanding, more patient, and more present. We remember what it felt like not to be understood, and from there, real communication begins.

We all know that talking to teenagers isn't always straightforward. They might not say much, or say it in a way that sounds like they don't care. But behind the sighs, the sarcasm, and the silences, there's a whole emotional world. Understanding this world takes intention and effort.

In this chapter, we'll explore what it really means to communicate with your teen, not from a place of control, but from a place of connection. We'll dive into tools that help open the door: active listening, creating safe spaces for conversation, and knowing when to talk and when to hold space.

And as you read through this chapter, remember that communicating with your teen isn't about getting every word right. It's about showing up with warmth, respect, and a willingness to see the world through their eyes, even just a little.

Listening versus Hearing

Let's talk about something pretty powerful—the art of *really* listening. Not just hearing the words, but actually tuning in and really understanding what's going on.

Picture this: your teen flops onto the couch after school, phone in hand. You ask how their day was, and all you get is a quick, "fine." Seems like a simple, surface-level exchange, right? But if you pay attention, there's a whole silent conversation happening. The slouch, the quiet tone, no eye contact, those are the subtle signals giving you a glimpse into what they're actually feeling. Maybe they bombed a test, had a fight with a friend, or are just buried in school stress. It's like they're speaking in a quiet emotional code, and if you're really listening, you'll catch it.

Now, when they *do* start talking, maybe about why they skipped out on chores or came home late, try this small but powerful move: reflect their words back to them in your own way. If they say, "I couldn't do the dishes, I had to study for a test," you might respond, "Okay, so studying took priority and the dishes didn't get done."

Why does this help? It shows them you're not just half-listening, you're genuinely trying to understand. It also gives them a chance to clarify if you misunderstood something. It's like asking them indirectly, "Is this what you meant?" It keeps the conversation open and clear.

And here's another thing—avoid interrupting. Even if you want to jump in with advice or your own take, hold off and let them finish. That small act of patience shows respect, and it makes them far more likely to keep sharing.

In a world full of noise and distractions, real listening can feel like a lost art. But especially with teens, it's a skill that makes a difference, switching scattered exchanges to real conversations. You'll build trust, strengthen your connection, and create a space where they feel heard and safe.

Navigating Teenage Time Bombs

Identifying Triggers

Picture this: it's a calm afternoon, and you casually ask your teen to help out with a few chores. Suddenly, there's an explosion: raised voices, eye rolls, maybe even a door slam. This is the unpredictable world of teenage melt-downs: what we might call "teenage time bombs." And like with any ticking device, the key to avoiding detonation is knowing what sets it off.

These emotional flare-ups don't happen randomly. They're often sparked by very specific triggers: academic stress, social pressures, or even things that seem small to us, like a delayed Wi-Fi connection or an offhand comment about their laundry. It's important to remember that what feels minor to you might feel huge to them. Their world is intense, and their emotional landscape is still under construction.

Start by paying close attention to patterns. Does tension rise around exam time? After hanging out with certain friends? When they haven't had enough sleep? These patterns can reveal the stress points that make your teen more vulnerable to emotional outbursts.

Understanding these triggers doesn't mean we can prevent every blow-up, but it does give us a powerful tool—empathy. When we know what's underneath the surface, we're better prepared to respond with calm and compassion instead of frustration.

Now, let's break down some of the most common triggers and how to navigate them:

- ## Academic Stress

We had covered this in detail earlier, but it's worth mentioning as a possible trigger. Exam season, with its looming deadlines and mounting pressure, is a major trigger for many teens. The fear of failure and the intense expectations—whether from themselves, school, or home—can feel overwhelming. When the stakes feel high, even a small academic hiccup can spark a big emotional reaction.

- ## Social Dynamics

Friendships during adolescence can be a minefield. A comment taken the wrong way, feeling excluded, peer pressure, or drama within a friend group can create a swirl of emotions. Since social belonging is so important at this stage, anything that threatens that sense of connection can easily become a trigger.

- **<u>Emotional Exhaustion</u>**

Teenagers often juggle more than we realize—school, friendships, home responsibilities, identity struggles, and sometimes even part-time jobs or family issues. Over time, this can lead to emotional burnout. Without enough downtime or emotional space to process everything, even a small frustration can push them over the edge.

As parents or educators, recognizing patterns—like tension around certain subjects, shifts in behavior before exams, or signs of sleep deprivation—can help us step in with support before things escalate.

Encouraging breaks, offering a calm listening ear, and helping create a balanced routine can go a long way.

Calm and Composed Responses

When faced with these emotional explosions, resist the urge to match anger with anger. Fire fuels fire, escalating the conflict. Instead, respond with calmness and composure. Maintain a serene demeanor, not to suppress your emotions, but to manage them effectively. This creates a safe space where your teen feels heard, not attacked. Take a deep breath, keep your voice steady, and address the behavior without criticism.

Let's say you're a teacher, and during a class discussion, a student named Becky unexpectedly expresses frustration about the difficulty of the topic, resulting in a heated outburst. In this situation, the initial reaction might be to meet Becky's frustration with your frustration, creating a potentially volatile atmosphere in the classroom. However, applying the principle of calm and composed responses can significantly alter the dynamics:

Recognizing the Trigger

First, acknowledge that the challenging topic triggered Becky emotional response. It could be academic stress or a struggle to comprehend the material.

Calm and Composed Reaction

Instead of reacting with frustration or irritation, respond with calmness and composure. Keep your voice steady, take a moment to collect your thoughts, and then address Becky's concerns.

Empathetic Listening

Create a safe space by actively listening to Becky's frustrations. This doesn't mean agreeing with everything she says, but rather demonstrating that her feelings are acknowledged and respected.

Problem-Solving Approach

Whenever emotions run high, try to gently guide the moment toward problem-solving. Talk through the situation together and explore possible ways to handle it. Offer your support without judgment. Responding with calm and steadiness doesn't mean brushing feelings aside—it means helping your teen manage them in a healthier way.

This kind of response creates a safe, supportive environment where they feel heard and understood. It also models emotional regulation in action, showing them how to face challenges constructively rather than reactively.

Let's continue with our earlier example involving Becky. After she reacts with frustration during a challenging lesson, and you've responded with calm and empathy, the next step is to guide the moment toward a solution together.

Here's how that can look in practice:

Acknowledging Emotions

Begin by validating what Becky is feeling. This doesn't mean agreeing with everything she says—it just means showing her that her emotions are understood. You might say, *"I can see this topic is really frustrating right now. It's okay to feel overwhelmed—these moments happen to all of us."*

This kind of acknowledgment helps her feel seen rather than shut down.

Transition to Problem-Solving

Once her emotions have been acknowledged, gently pivot the conversation. A calm, open-ended question can do wonders: *"Do you want to talk about which part is feeling the hardest right now?"* or *"What do you think would make this feel more manageable?"* This shifts the focus from what went wrong to what can be done next.

Offering Strategies

Collaboratively explore possible ways forward. You might suggest:

- Breaking the task into smaller, more doable steps

- Revisiting earlier material she felt confident with

- Using visual aids, summaries, or examples that match her learning style

By brainstorming together, you're showing her how to move from stuck to supported without judgment.

Extra Help

Offer additional support if she needs more time or space to work through the material. You could say:

"If it would help, we can go over this one-on-one later, or I can give you some extra examples to try at your own pace."

This makes it clear that support is available without pressure.

Encourage Self-Advocacy

Remind her that asking for help is a strength, not a weakness. Try something like:

"If this happens again, don't be afraid to speak up—I'd rather we work through it together than let it build up."

You're reinforcing that her voice matters and that she has agency in the learning process.

Express Support

Close the conversation with a note of encouragement. Let her know you're on her side.

"You're not alone in this—I'm here to help you figure it out, and I believe you can."

Even a small, genuine comment like that can build a sense of safety and confidence.

This way, you're not just managing the moment; you're modeling emotional intelligence and resilience in real time. It's this kind of support that teaches them how to face challenges without fear and ask for help without shame.

Post-Conflict Resolution Follow-Ups

The resolution of a conflict isn't the end; what comes next matters just as much. Following up after the moment has passed gives teens a chance to reflect, process, and feel truly heard. Think of it as a quiet debrief after a storm: a time to check in, make sense of what happened, and consider what could be done differently next time.

Take Becky, for instance. After her emotional outburst and your calm, problem-solving conversation, things may have settled down. But don't let it end there. Maybe the next day, during a neutral moment, between classes, during lunch, or even just while walking out together, you gently check in:

Acknowledging the Resolution

Start by recognizing the effort she put into moving forward.

"Hey, I really appreciated how open you were yesterday. That took a lot of maturity."

This shows you noticed her growth, not just the disruption.

Transitioning to a Follow-Up Conversation

Keep the tone light and natural. No pressure, just curiosity and care.

"How did you feel about how we handled things yesterday? Did you find it helpful?"

Here, you're inviting her to reflect, not revisit the conflict.

Reflecting on the Experience

Ask open-ended questions that let her lead the reflection.

"Is there anything you'd do differently next time? Anything I could do differently?"

You're showing her that conflict resolution is a shared process, not a top-down directive.

Planning for Next Time

Discussing adjustments helps her feel more in control of future situations.

"If something like that comes up again, what would help you stay grounded?"

Maybe it's a signal word, a short break, or just knowing she won't be judged for having a tough moment.

Validating Her Feelings

Above all, remind her that her emotions are valid, even if the way they come out sometimes needs work.

"It's okay to have big feelings. What matters is how we move through them—and I'm here for that."

<u>Turning Conflict into Growth</u>

Let her know that these kinds of check-ins aren't about revisiting drama; they're about learning together. When teens know that their emotional moments won't be held against them, they start to feel safer and more open in the future.

Note that Becky's example can also be applied to parent-child relationships, not just teacher-student ones.

The Empathy Bridge

One of the most powerful ways to connect with your teen, especially during emotionally charged moments, is through empathy. When your teen is hurting, frustrated, or overwhelmed, they're not necessarily looking for solutions. What they often crave most is simple human understanding. They want to know they're not alone in what they're feeling. This is where building an "empathy bridge" comes in—small, intentional moments where you meet them emotionally, right where they are.

Let's see how you can do this in everyday moments:

Validating Feelings

Let's say your teen approaches you, upset that they didn't make the school basketball team. The natural instinct might be to comfort them with a hopeful, "You'll get it next year," or offer advice on what to improve. But what they often need first isn't reassurance—it's validation. A simple acknowledgment like, *"That must feel really disappointing. I can see how much this meant to you,"* goes a long way.

Validation says, *"I hear you. I see you. Your feelings are real, and they matter."* It's not about agreeing with everything they say or do; it's about honoring their emotional experience. Even if you can't fix the situation, showing that you understand how they feel builds trust and makes them more likely to open up again next time.

Sharing Personal Experiences

Another way to strengthen that bridge of empathy is by gently sharing your own experiences. When appropriate, opening up about times when you've felt let down or faced rejection helps normalize their emotions. Maybe you can recall a moment when you didn't get a job you really wanted, or when a big plan fell through.

Say something like, *"I remember being so crushed when I didn't get into the college I was hoping for. I know it's not the same, but I get what that kind of disappointment feels like."*

The point isn't to shift the focus to yourself, but to show them that you've been there, too.

Empathetic Responses

When your teen shares something difficult, resist the urge to jump into problem-solving mode. Instead, pause and reflect their feelings back with empathy. If they're upset about a fight with a friend, try: *"That sounds really painful. I can imagine you're feeling hurt and confused."*

Empathy says, *"I may not have all the answers, but I'm here with you."* It's about being emotionally present, not necessarily to fix, but to feel with them. These responses create a safe space where your teen knows they won't be dismissed, lectured, or rushed through their feelings.

You don't need dramatic speeches or the "right" words to build an empathy bridge. It's the small, consistent moments that add up. Each time you respond with presence and compassion, you lay down another brick. Over time, that bridge becomes strong enough to carry your connection through even the most turbulent teenage years.

Chapter 7

Discipline and Boundaries

Guiding Your Teen With Empathy and Consistency

*"Our boundaries define our personal space –
and we need to be sovereign there in order
to be able to step into our full power and
potential."* ~Jessica Moore

J essica Moore's words beautifully capture what lies at the heart of healthy discipline and boundaries during the teen years. At its core, this is about more than just rules; it's about helping our teenagers feel safe enough to grow and strong enough to thrive.

Boundaries, when set with care and clarity, create a framework of trust and respect. They help define personal space, not to restrict or control, but to give room for autonomy and healthy development. For teenagers, whose brains are still learning how to self-regulate and make decisions, clear and respectful boundaries are the scaffolding for independence. They give teens something steady to push against as they figure out who they are.

That's where empathy comes in. It's not just about laying down rules—it's about listening to your teen's perspective and honoring their emotional world while still maintaining your role as a guide. Empathy doesn't mean letting go of structure; it means enforcing it in a way that respects the teenager's voice and humanity. It's saying, *"I hear you, and I understand, but here's why this boundary matters."*

Just as important as empathy is consistency. Boundaries that change from day to day or are enforced only when we're tired or angry send mixed messages. Teens need to know what to expect. When limits are predictable and fair, it creates stability, and from that, a sense of security. Even when they push back (and they will), consistency reassures them that the world around them isn't shifting beneath their feet.

In this chapter, we'll see how to guide teens with a combination of empathy and firmness. We'll look at how setting boundaries can actually strengthen your connection rather than weaken it and how consistent, respectful discipline builds the inner scaffolding your teen needs to step confidently into their power and potential.

Setting Boundaries and Building Consistency for Growth

Clear Expectations

Provide specific, detailed guidelines for tasks like chores, homework, curfew, and screen time.

Instead of vague instructions, offer clear and detailed expectations. For example, "Wash the dishes every evening after dinner and take out the trash every Tuesday and Friday morning."

Involvement and Collaboration

Involve your teenager in the process of setting expectations.

Encourage a conversation about what's reasonable, negotiable, and non-negotiable. This collaborative approach fosters a sense of value and increases their willingness to adhere to the rules.

Consistency as the Backbone

Now, let's talk about the backbone of it all – consistency. Without it, your efforts will be futile. Make sure to enforce rules consistently to avoid confusion or rule-bending. For instance, if washing dishes is a daily routine, stick to it consistently, not just when it's convenient.

Address Rule Violations Promptly

Promptly address any rule violations, irrespective of external factors.

Consistent enforcement sends a strong message about the importance of rules and the need for respect.

Regular Revisions

As your teenager matures, regularly revise and update boundaries.

Adjust rules to reflect your teen's growing maturity and expanding responsibilities. This ongoing process respects their evolving individuality and maintains a harmonious living environment.

This isn't about letting go of all the rules; it's about adjusting to make sure the rules still apply.

Deliberate and Thoughtful Construction

Each boundary is a deliberate and thoughtful construction.

It lays the foundation for a healthy parent-teenager relationship by shaping their understanding of respect, responsibility, and the value of clear guidelines.

Overall, setting boundaries isn't about power plays or strict rules; it's about building a clear, consistent, and adaptable framework to guide your teenager's behavior.

Navigating the Discipline Dilemma

When parenting teenagers, the age-old adage "Spare the rod, spoil the child" may not hold water. Dealing with teenage misbehavior requires a nuanced and empathetic approach — a shift from punishment to consequences.

Natural Consequences

- Scenario: Your teenager consistently forgets to set their alarm, leading to waking up late and missing the bus. Instead of a reprimand, consider letting natural consequences unfold. They miss the bus; they must figure out alternative travel, facing any repercussions from the school administration.

- Essence: Natural consequences provide learning opportunities, allowing teenagers to understand that their choices have consequences.

Logical Consequences

- Scenario: Your teenager borrows your car without asking and gets a speeding ticket. Instead of solely relying on natural consequences, implement logical consequences. For instance, temporarily restrict their driving privileges or have them pay the ticket from their savings.

- Essence: Logical consequences are directly linked to misbehavior, but implemented by you — they are respectful, relevant, and realistic.

Avoiding Punitive Measures

In the heat of the moment, punitive measures like grounding or taking away privileges may be tempting.

- Concern: Punitive measures can breed resentment, damage your relationship, and fail to teach your teen about responsibility and decision-making.

- Alternative: Instead of punishing, focus on teaching. Use misbehavior as a teaching moment, guiding your teen towards better choices.

The Power of Choice

By allowing natural and logical consequences to unfold, you empower your teen to make choices and be accountable for them.

- Message: "I trust you to make decisions and handle the consequences." This fosters responsibility, boosts self-esteem, and enhances decision-making skills.

- Role: Your role is not to control but to guide, support, and allow freedom for learning from choices.

Discipline as a Learning Journey

Navigating teen discipline can be simple.

- Approach: Focus on natural and logical consequences, avoid punitive measures, and foster choice and accountability.

- Outcome: Transform discipline complications into a learning journey that shapes behavior and strengthens your relationship with your teen.

Navigating Defiance

When it comes to parenting teens, few things can feel more frustrating—or more personal—than dealing with defiance. It's one of those challenges that can catch you off guard, even when you think you're prepared. It's like caring for a wilting plant: the leaves droop, the color fades, and nothing seems to help. But the real fix doesn't lie in trimming the edges; it lies in getting to the roots.

Understanding the Root Cause

Defiance in teens is rarely just about the surface behavior. Sometimes, it's a cry for independence. Other times, it's about pushing boundaries, expressing bottled-up frustration, or trying to feel heard. And quite often, as we saw earlier, there's something else simmering beneath: school stress, social drama, or a growing sense of feeling misunderstood or overwhelmed.

When we take the time to look past the behavior and ask what's driving it, we can stop reacting and start responding with intention.

Responding Without Escalating

Defiance can easily turn into a tug-of-war—one where both sides dig in, and no one really wins. When your teen pushes, your first instinct might be to push back. But what if you didn't? What if, instead of grabbing the rope tighter, you simply let go?

Staying calm in those heated moments isn't easy, but it's powerful. It shows your teen that you're not there to battle them—you're there to understand. Taking a deep breath, speaking gently, and focusing on the behavior (not their character) can shift the entire energy of the conversation.

Using "I" statements can also go a long way. Rather than saying, *"You're being rude,"* try something like, *"I feel dismissed when my requests are ignored."* This small shift takes the sting out of confrontation and opens the door to actual connection. It invites your teen into the conversation instead of pushing them further away.

When to Seek Professional Help

There are times when love, patience, and calm communication still don't seem to be enough—and that's okay.

Just like you'd call in a gardener if your entire garden was struggling, it's completely valid to seek help if your teen's behavior seems overwhelming or persistent. If defiance is showing up alongside aggression, risky behavior, or signs of depression or self-harm, it's time to consider involving a professional.

Therapists and counselors can offer a neutral, supportive space for your teen to unpack what they're going through. More importantly, they can equip both you and your teen with tools to navigate tough moments in healthier, more constructive ways.

As a parent or caregiver, it's important to note that reaching out for help isn't a sign of failure—it's an act of strength. It means you're doing everything in your power to support your teen, even if it means letting someone else take the reins.

Opportunities for Growth and Connection

While defiance can feel like a brick wall, it can also be a doorway to deepen your connection. These challenges, hard as they may be, offer us the chance to show up for our teens—not with lectures or ultimatums, but with steadiness, empathy, and presence. They are opportunities for you to reinforce your love, model emotional regulation, and remind your teen that they're not alone, even when things feel tense or messy.

Next, we'll shift our focus to another key part of their world—academics. We've touched on this a bit in previous chapters as a stressor. However, here we will explore how the teenage brain processes learning, what fuels or hinders motivation, and how we can support their academic journey in a way that feels grounded, healthy, and empowering.

Chapter 8

The Learning Scope

Helping Your Teen Towards Academic Success

"Only those who dare to fail greatly can ever achieve greatly." – Robert F. Kennedy

As a parent helping your teen navigate the ups and downs of academic life, these words from Robert F. Kennedy hold powerful truth. They are a reminder we all need sometimes, especially when we're watching our teens wrestle with pressure, setbacks, and the constant demand to succeed.

The path to academic success can be messy. It includes late nights, missed marks, second tries, and unexpected detours. And that's okay. In fact, it's more than okay; it's essential. The ability to take risks, to try and fail and try again, is what builds not just knowledge, but confidence, resilience, and grit. Your teen may stumble, yes—but those stumbles often become the very ground they'll rise from.

One of the most meaningful gifts you can give your teenager is permission to fail. Not the kind of failure that comes from carelessness; but the kind that comes from pushing their boundaries, challenging themselves, and daring to try something new. Whether it's taking on a difficult subject, experimenting with a different study method, or simply asking for help when they're stuck, these moments are where real growth happens.

Reframing failure as part of the learning process—not as something to fear, but something to learn from—is key. It allows your teen to see challenges not as dead ends but as stepping stones. It also signals to them that success isn't just about grades; it's about perseverance, curiosity, and learning.

This chapter dives into just that: how to support your teen through the academic journey with encouragement, strategy, and heart. We'll look at how motivation works, what drives learning, and how you can help them stay focused and resilient, even when things get hard.

And let's be real, motivation isn't always easy to come by, even for adults. That's why understanding what fuels your teen matters. One big driver? Intrinsic motivation. This is that inner spark that lights up when they're doing something because they genuinely enjoy it or find meaning in it. For them, it might be the thrill of solving a tough math problem, the satisfaction of finishing a great book, or that feeling of pride when they finally understand a tricky science concept.

These are the moments we want to nurture—not through pressure, but through support and encouragement.

How Can Parents Help?

Well, let me share with you some tips below:

- **Be a Learning Ally**

Act as a learning ally for your teenager. Show interest in what they're studying, ask about their projects, and be there to answer questions or help when they're stuck. When they see that you're genuinely interested, it can boost their motivation.

- ## Create a Study Routine

Help your teenager establish a study routine. Consistency is key. Having a set time and place for studying can make it a habit, and habits are easier to stick with. Make sure they have a quiet and comfortable space to focus.

- ## Explore Different Learning Styles

People learn in different ways. Some are visual learners, some prefer reading, and others learn by doing. Figure out your teen's learning style and encourage them to use techniques that suit them best. This could include visual aids, flashcards, or hands-on activities.

- ## Encourage Breaks and Self-Care

Studying for long hours without breaks can lead to burnout. Encourage your teenager to take short breaks, stretch, or do something enjoyable between study sessions. Taking care of their well-being is crucial for long-term success.

- ## Connect Learning to Real Life

Help your teen see the real-world applications of what they're learning. Whether it's math, science, or literature, show them how these subjects relate to everyday life.

Understanding the practical aspects can make studying more meaningful and interesting.

- **Offer Choices and Autonomy**

Allow your teenager to have a say in their learning. Offer them choices when possible, like letting them pick a topic for a project or decide how to approach a particular assignment. Autonomy can increase their sense of responsibility and motivation.

- **Seek External Support**

If your teenager is struggling with a particular subject, consider seeking external support. This could be a tutor, a study group, or online resources. Sometimes, a different perspective or additional help can make a significant difference.

- **Set a Positive Example**

Children often learn by example. If they see you valuing learning, setting goals, and celebrating your achievements, it sets a positive tone. Share your own experiences of overcoming challenges and emphasize the importance of continuous learning.

Remember, the key is to create a supportive and engaging environment where learning is seen as a positive and rewarding experience. By incorporating these additional points, you're setting the stage for your teenager's academic success and fostering a lifelong love of learning.

Smart Work Over Hard Work

Not all effort is created equal, and when it comes to schoolwork, the secret isn't always working harder, but working smarter. Many teens believe that long hours spent bent over a book equals success, but what really matters is *how* they study. This is where you, as a parent, can make a meaningful difference.

Helping your teen develop effective study habits doesn't mean micromanaging their homework. It means guiding them toward techniques that not only make learning more manageable but also more enjoyable.

For instance:

Effective Note-Taking

Taking notes isn't just about copying everything the teacher says. It's about picking out the most important ideas and capturing them in a way that actually makes sense to the learner. Encourage your teen to experiment with different note-taking methods, whether it's outlining ideas in a sequence, using the Cornell Method (dividing the page into keywords, notes, and a summary), or drawing out mind maps.

The goal is for their notes to reflect how *they* understand the topic, not just how it was presented. Support them by asking questions like, *"Which method helps you remember better?"* or *"Want to show me how you organized that tricky topic?"* Even this simple interest from you reinforces the value of finding a system that works.

Remind them, too, that notes aren't just for storing information—they're tools for making connections. Encourage them to highlight, doodle, rephrase ideas in their own words—anything that brings the material to life. Their notebook doesn't need to be perfect—it needs to make sense to *them*.

Active Recall

Passive review—just re-reading notes—only goes so far. Active recall, on the other hand, is a game-changer. It's like watching a mystery movie and trying to remember the clues without rewinding. It requires the brain to work a little harder, and that's exactly what helps the learning stick.

Encourage your teen to quiz themselves, summarize what they've just learned out loud, or even explain it to you as if they were teaching a class. (Bonus: this can be a fun way to connect, too.) Flashcards are a great tool here, as is turning headings in their notes into questions.

Spaced Repetition

You know how watering a plant once a month won't keep it alive, but a little bit every few days does the trick? The same goes for studying. Spaced repetition is the habit of reviewing material over increasing intervals, rather than cramming it all in the night before a test.

Help your teen build this rhythm by checking in after they've learned something new. Maybe say, *"Hey, want to do a quick review of what you covered yesterday?"* Then revisit it again a few days later. There are even apps that can help space out review sessions based on how well your teen remembers each item.

By revisiting content over time, their brain has a better chance of turning short-term knowledge into long-term understanding.

Time Management

One of the biggest hurdles teens face isn't always the material itself; it's knowing how to manage their time. You can help by guiding them to break their work into smaller, doable chunks. Sit down together and create a flexible schedule that makes space for each subject, built around realistic goals and built-in breaks.

Techniques like the Pomodoro Method—25 minutes of focused work followed by a 5-minute break—can make studying feel less overwhelming. And remember, time off *is* part of smart work. Encourage them to step away from the screen, take a walk, stretch, or grab a snack.

Rather than enforcing a strict timetable, help them build a relationship with time that feels empowering instead of draining.

The Failure Fallacy

Growth Mindset

We often think of failure as the opposite of success, but in reality, it's one of the most powerful tools for learning. Helping your teen embrace a *growth mindset* means encouraging them to see intelligence and ability not as fixed traits, but as things they can develop with effort, time, and persistence.

A growth mindset invites your teen to look at challenges and setbacks as stepping stones, not signs that they're "not good enough," but proof that they're learning and growing. Instead of saying, "I failed the test," they can begin to say, "I didn't do well this time, but I'll learn from it and do better next time." It's a subtle shift, but one that can completely change how they view themselves and their potential.

Seeing Mistakes as Opportunities

When your teen stumbles during a class presentation or struggles with a tough subject, their first instinct might be frustration or self-doubt. This is where you can gently step in and help reframe the moment. Mistakes aren't proof of failure—they're part of the process.

You might say something like, *"Okay, that didn't go the way you hoped—but what do you think you could try differently next time?"* Over time, they'll learn that one misstep doesn't define them. It's just feedback for their next step.

Constructive Feedback

Feedback is powerful—but how it's delivered makes all the difference. Try to focus less on the outcome ("You got an A!") and more on the process that got them there. Say things like, *"You put in consistent study time and stayed focused—that really paid off."*

When they're struggling, offer feedback that's specific and supportive rather than vague or critical. Instead of *"You need to do better,"* try, *"I noticed you got stuck on the last few questions—let's figure out where it got confusing and work through it together."*

This kind of feedback shows them that learning is a process, and improvement is always possible.

Building Resilience

Sometimes, things don't go as planned—and that's okay. What matters most is how your teen bounces back. Resilience is what helps them push through frustration, setbacks, or even failure, and keep moving forward.

Help them develop resilience by normalizing struggle. Remind them it's okay to feel disappointed—but it's also okay to start again. Teach simple tools like taking a break, deep breathing, or walking away for a moment and coming back with fresh eyes (review our section on resilience for more tips on how to do this). Encourage them to ask for help—from teachers, peers, or even you—when they're stuck.

Remember that when you support your teen in developing a growth mindset, you're not just helping them succeed in school. You're helping them build the emotional and mental tools they'll need for life.

Chapter 9

The Invisible Battles of Adolescence

Body Image, Peer Pressure, and Impulsivity

"To lose confidence in one's body is to lose confidence in oneself." ~Simone de Beauvoir.

During the teenage years, when so much of a young person's identity is still taking shape, this quote really hits hard. Adolescence is a time of massive physical, emotional, and social shifts. As teens become more aware of how they look and how they're perceived, their relationship with their body can start to define how they feel about themselves as a whole.

Body image can become a quiet battlefield. Teens are constantly bombarded with messages, online, at school, and even from friends, about what's considered "good enough." And when those standards feel out of reach, it's not just about appearances anymore. Their confidence, sense of identity, and self-worth can take a hit too.

Then there's peer pressure. It's not always loud or evident; it can be subtle, like the pressure to dress a certain way, follow certain trends, or keep up with filtered versions of reality they see on social media. The desire to fit in during this time is so strong, and for some teens, this desire can override their better judgment or push them into decisions that don't align with who they truly are.

Now, when you add impulsivity to the mix, it's easy to see how quickly things can snowball. One impulsive choice, made in the heat of wanting to be accepted or seen, can lead to unhealthy habits like crash dieting, excessive exercising, or even riskier behaviors.

But teens don't have to fight these battles alone. As parents, caregivers, and educators, we can be their safe harbor; the place where they learn to see their body with kindness, where their worth isn't tied to how they look, and where fitting in doesn't mean losing themselves. We can start by having real conversations about body image and self-acceptance. We can help them question unrealistic standards and tune into what makes them unique.

The goal isn't to shield them from the world—they'll face pressures, no doubt—but to equip them with the tools and self-awareness to move through it without losing their grounding. Helping them build a positive, respectful relationship with their body doesn't just boost confidence—it lays the groundwork for a strong, steady sense of self that can weather the ups and downs of adolescence and beyond.

Let's see how to do this in this chapter:

Navigating the Teen Body Image Maze—For Parents

We know that being a teenager is like being in a funhouse mirror maze – nothing looks quite right, everything feels exaggerated, and it's easy to get disoriented. On top of juggling school, friendships, and growing responsibilities, your teen is also trying to figure out how they feel about their body—and that's no small feat in a world constantly telling them how they *should* look.

As a parent, it can be hard to know how to help. But here's the good news: you don't need to have all the answers. You just need a few solid tools and the willingness to stay in the conversation. Think of this as a heart-to-heart over coffee (or tea), where we unpack three powerful ways to support your teen through the body image maze: media literacy, positive self-talk, and the impact of representation and role models.

Media Literacy

Social media is like a non-stop slideshow of seemingly perfect bodies, flawless faces, and jet-setting lifestyles. But here's the deal: those images are often as real as unicorns. Media literacy is like putting on reality-check glasses; it helps your teen see behind the polished façade.

What can you do?

Teach your teen to question what they see on social media. Explain how photo editing apps create fantasy, and how advertising preys on insecurities to sell products. Make them media-savvy so they can look at these images with a critical eye. This empowers them to appreciate diversity, knowing that worth isn't determined by appearance.

Positive Self-Talk

What your teen says to themselves matters a lot. This internal dialogue is called self-talk, and it's a powerful tool in building a positive body image.

What can you do?

Encourage positive self-talk. Help your teen recognize and replace negative thoughts with affirmations that focus on strengths, abilities, and character rather than just appearance. Remind them that everyone is unique, with qualities that go beyond physical looks. This builds a foundation for self-acceptance and self-love.

Role Models and Representation

Positive role models are those who reflect diverse, realistic, and unaltered bodies and appearances. These role models, both in real life and the media, provide a counter-narrative to the narrow beauty standards bombarding your teen.

What can you do?

Encourage your teen to find role models who celebrate body positivity, diversity, and self-acceptance. It could be athletes emphasizing strength and health over appearance, celebrities speaking out against body shaming, or influencers sharing unedited photos. These role models show that beauty isn't confined to a particular size or shape, and looks don't determine success.

Navigating the Peer Pressure Puzzle-For Parents

In this part of our book, we'll tackle the social maze of peer pressure. Teenagers face a horde of influences, and it's essential to equip them with the right tools to navigate these challenging waters.

Assertiveness Skills

Assertiveness helps your teen stand up for themselves while respecting others. This skill involves expressing feelings, opinions, and needs confidently. It's like giving your teen a sturdy boat to navigate through the waves of peer pressure.

What can you do?

Guide your teenager to communicate assertively. Practice scenarios together, like saying no to risky behaviors or standing up against bullying. Reinforce that it's absolutely okay to go against the crowd and express disagreement respectfully. Like any skill, assertiveness improves with practice.

Choosing Friends Wisely

Encourage your teen to be mindful of their friends—do these friends respect their values? Are they accepted for who they are? True friendships uplift; they don't bring anyone down.

What can you do?

Ask reflective questions. Are their friends positively influencing them? Do these friendships contribute to their growth? Urge your teen to hold onto friendships that value authenticity and mutual growth. Remind them that friendships should never compromise their values or well-being.

Family Values and Personal Beliefs

Family values provide guidance in the vastness of adolescence. Engage in open discussions about your family values, such as honesty, respect, responsibility, and compassion. Explain why these values matter and how they can steer your teen's decisions.

What can you do?

Encourage your teen to reflect on their personal beliefs. What do they stand for? What principles guide their actions? This introspection strengthens their moral compass, helping them navigate peer pressure without losing sight of their values.

Guiding Teens Through Impulsivity

Now, let's talk about helping your teens hit the brakes on impulsivity and cruise through life with a bit more control and patience:

Delayed Gratification

Picture your teen scrolling through their favorite online store. They've just spotted a pair of sneakers they really want—but they've also been saving up for something bigger, like concert tickets or a new phone. Now they're stuck in that classic tug-of-war: do they hit "Buy Now" for that quick thrill, or keep saving for the thing they've been dreaming about?

Choosing the latter is where delayed gratification comes to life. It's not about denying pleasure altogether; it's about learning when to pause, weigh the options, and hold out for something more meaningful. And in today's world of instant everything, helping your teen build this skill is a powerful step toward long-term resilience and self-control.

What can you do?

Start simple. Engage your teen in activities that require waiting, like baking a cake. Waiting for it to bake and cool before diving in is a small lesson in patience. As they get better at waiting, introduce larger goals that demand more extended periods of self-control. This cultivates patience, stress management, and better decision-making.

Role-Playing Scenarios

Let's say your teen wants to attend a late-night party, and you're concerned about their safety. You can switch gears and role-play this scenario together. Take turns playing both sides.

This exercise helps your teen explore different ways to handle situations, express their thoughts and feelings, and understand your perspective.

Navigating the Dark Side of the Internet

The digital world is expansive, and as expected, not all online interactions are friendly. There's a shadowy side—an alleyway concealed where cyberbullying lurks. This form of bullying takes place behind screen names and profile pictures, making it challenging to detect.

Recognizing Signs of Cyberbullying

If your teenager appears distressed after using their devices, becomes secretive about online activities, or exhibits changes in behavior like withdrawing from friends and family, it might be a sign of cyberbullying. Other indicators include alterations in eating or sleeping patterns, declining grades, or sudden disinterest in school.

Impact on Mental Health

Cyberbullying triggers feelings of sadness, fear, and loneliness. It can lead to a struggle to focus, with hurtful comments or threatening messages lingering in their thoughts. The impact on mental health can be profound, potentially causing or exacerbating issues like anxiety, depression, and even suicidal thoughts.

In the next section, we will see the effects of adolescent pressures in action and how to go around them.

Case Studies and Solutions

Real-World Challenges

Cyberbullying

Consider Ben, a high school sophomore targeted by an anonymous online hate page. Recognizing the signs, Ben's parents took swift action, reporting the incident to the school and the social media platform. Professional counseling helped Ben navigate the emotional distress, emphasizing the importance of open communication, prompt action, and seeking professional help.

Academic Pressure

In Lisa's case, intense academic pressure led to panic attacks. Intervention from her parents and a school counselor provided stress management techniques, emphasizing the need for a balanced approach to academics, prioritizing learning over grades and well-being over achievements.

Substance Abuse

Andrew's early experimentation with drugs was met with calm but decisive intervention from his parents. They reached out for professional support and enrolled him in a peer support group.

His story highlights the importance of early intervention, professional help, and peer support in dealing with teenage substance abuse.

Mental Health Issues

On the other hand, Nina battled depression, concealed by typical teenage behavior. Recognizing the signs, Nina's family sought professional help. This emphasizes the importance of recognizing mental health issues, seeking professional help, and providing a supportive home environment.

As we move on to the next chapter, let's hold on to one thing: every challenge is a chance to connect with our teens, regardless of how "bad" the situation may seem.

Chapter 10

Embracing Uniqueness

Navigating the Spectrum of Individual Differences in Adolescents

"Every one of us is different in some way, but for those of us who are more different, we have to put more effort into convincing the less different that we can do the same thing they can, just differently." — Marlee Matlin

While everyone is different in their own way, those who stand out a little more, whether due to a disability, neurodivergence, cultural background, or any other reason, often carry the extra emotional labor of proving they belong. Not by changing who they are, but by showing that they too can thrive, just in their own way.

When it comes to teenagers, this truth takes on even more weight. Adolescence is a time of exploration, identity-shaping, and comparison. It's when many young people start to feel the pressure to fit into predefined boxes; boxes that may not have been made with them in mind. That's why creating a space where they feel accepted for who they *truly* are becomes not just helpful, but essential.

As parents, educators, and caregivers, part of our job is helping teens embrace their individuality, not as something to overcome, but as something to be proud of. It's about showing them that different doesn't mean less. That success doesn't have one look, one path, or one speed. And that their unique ways of thinking, learning, expressing, and being are not only valid, but valuable.

Fostering this kind of inclusive mindset starts with simple, consistent actions: listening without judgment, celebrating effort over comparison, and reminding teens that there are many ways to be smart, talented, kind, and capable. When we create a culture where differences are welcomed and respected, we offer our teenagers the freedom to grow into the fullest version of themselves without needing to shrink or stretch to meet someone else's expectations.

Let's see how:

Embracing Individuality

Here, we'll take a closer look at what it means to be "normal" (hint: it's not one-size-fits-all). Teenagers aren't meant to be carbon copies of each other – they're a mix of temperaments, talents, quirks, and questions, each one unfolding in their own time. Appreciating their differences is necessary if we want to truly connect with and support them. Each teen is a one-of-a-kind masterpiece, still in the making.

Personality Traits

Teenagers, like stars in a vast sky, shine with distinct personality traits. Some may lean towards introversion, finding solace in quiet introspection, while others radiate extroversion, thriving in the energy of social interactions. When it comes to education, organizational wizards co-exist with spontaneous thinkers.

What can you do?

Appreciate these traits as windows into their world. By understanding their behavior, preferences, and interaction styles, we can guide them in a way that resonates with their unique personality.

Learning Styles

Just as we savor different tastes in music or food, teenagers have diverse learning styles. Visual learners absorb knowledge through images and diagrams, auditory learners thrive in discussions and lectures, while kinesthetic learners flourish through hands-on activities.

What can you do?

Recognize and embrace their learning style. Tailor teaching or parenting strategies to match their preferences, enriching their learning experience and enhancing understanding and retention of information.

Emotional Sensitivities

As we now understand, emotions in adolescence are unpredictable and diverse. Some teenagers experience emotions intensely, while others maintain a steady emotional landscape. Recognizing these emotional sensitivities allows us to understand their emotional climate and support them accordingly.

What can you do?

Acknowledge and validate their feelings. Understanding their emotional experiences enables us to provide the necessary support, manage emotional outbursts, and navigate conflicts with sensitivity.

Social Preferences

Teenagers, social explorers in their own right, showcase diverse social preferences. Some embrace large gatherings, while others seek comfort in intimate settings.

What can you do?

Consider social preferences as a roadmap to their social world. Respect their comfort zones, offer guidance in building positive social relationships, and provide support in overcoming social challenges. This knowledge unveils insights into their behavior, fostering a deeper connection.

Navigating Diverse Personality Types

When it comes to personalities, teenagers come with a rich category of traits. To guide them effectively, let's have a look at strategies tailored to different personality types:

Strategies for Introverted Teens

Introverted teenagers recharge through solitude, valuing depth in social interactions. Connect with introverted teens by respecting their need for personal space and quiet time. Avoid labeling them as shy, appreciate their reflective nature, and engage in meaningful one-on-one conversations. Also, support their deep interests, allowing their thoughts and ideas to speak volumes.

Strategies for Extroverted Teens

An extroverted teenager thrives in social circles, enjoying group activities and lively conversations. Embrace their social nature by providing opportunities for expression and engaging in stimulating discussions.

Encourage participation in group activities that align with their outgoing personality. While they seek external stimulation, help them find moments of quiet reflection, creating a balance between energetic social engagement and introspective solitude.

Strategies for Sensitive Teens

Sensitive teens are attuned to emotional nuances, empathetic, and deeply affected by others' feelings. Acknowledge their emotions without judgment, fostering a safe space for expression. Encourage creative outlets like art, music, or writing to channel their sensitivity positively. Make sure you recognize their strength in empathy and connection, so they are able to turn their emotional depth into a source of resilience and understanding.

Strategies for Assertive Teens

Assertive teens exude confidence, take initiative, and stand up for their beliefs. Respect their independence, supporting their self-expression and leadership qualities.

Where appropriate, provide constructive feedback and guide them in developing active listening skills and empathy. Take any chance you can get to channel their assertiveness positively, nurturing qualities that drive leadership, initiative, and positive change.

Case Study

Exploring the Impact of Individual Differences on Behavior

The Introverted Teen: Grace's Story

Grace is a 14-year-old introvert who cherishes alone time and thrives in one-on-one interactions. Grace's parents initially worried about her reserved nature, mistaking it for shyness or social anxiety.

Understanding the nuances of introversion, they came to appreciate Grace's deep reflective nature and her ability to connect on a profound level with a few close friends. Respecting her need for personal space, they supported her love for painting and reading, providing the joy and solitude she needed.

The Extroverted Teen: Liam's Journey

Liam, a 13-year-old extrovert, finds energy in social interactions and group activities. Initially, his parents found his constant need for social engagement exhausting. Recognizing this as part of his extroverted nature, they began to value his social skills and his knack for making friends easily.

Liam thrives when surrounded by people, and his parents support his extroverted tendencies by encouraging team sports and social events, providing the external stimulation he craves.

The Sensitive Teen: Maya's Emotional World

Maya, a 15-year-old with heightened emotional sensitivity, experiences emotions intensely. Her parents, initially overwhelmed by the depth of her reactions, learned to value her deep empathy and keen observance of others' feelings.

Recognizing Maya's rich inner life expressed through poetry, they supported her sensitivity by validating her emotions, creating a calm environment, and encouraging creative outlets for emotional expression.

The Assertive Teen: Ethan's Confidence Unleashed

Ethan, a 16-year-old assertive teenager, fearlessly expresses his thoughts and stands up for his beliefs. His parents initially found his assertiveness challenging, mistaking it for disobedience. Understanding his assertive nature, they learned to appreciate his self-confidence and leadership qualities.

Ethan takes initiative in group projects and stands up against bullying. His parents support his assertiveness by fostering open communication, respecting his opinions, and guiding him to balance assertiveness with active listening and empathy.

These case studies highlight the diverse experiences of teenagers, emphasizing that understanding and supporting them require a personalized approach.

One of the most rewarding parts of parenting a teenager is watching them come into their own. Discovering their unique strengths is all about being keen enough to notice the little things that light them up.

The key is to tune into what draws them in. A teen who's always humming a tune or writing lyrics might be exploring a creative path in music. One who patiently helps their younger sibling with homework could be showing early signs of becoming a future teacher or mentor. Our job is to notice these sparks and gently fan them, without any pressure.

Of course, part of supporting growth also means acknowledging the areas where they struggle. This isn't about pointing out flaws; it's about recognizing where they might need a bit more guidance. Confidence doesn't grow from praise alone; it comes from trying, stumbling, and realizing you can get back up.

As we turn the page to the next chapter, we'll see how you can build a strong, trusting, and lasting connection with your teen.

Chapter 11

BUILDING BRIDGES

Fostering a Meaningful Connection With Your Teen

"The way we talk to our children becomes their inner voice." — Peggy O'Mara

There's something quietly powerful in the way we speak to our teenagers. Our tone, our choice of words, even the pauses between them, often shape how our teens talk to themselves. Peggy O'Mara's quote reminds us that what we say today remains in our children's hearts tomorrow.

Fostering a meaningful connection with your teen is essential. While teens may not always say it out loud, what they crave most is to feel understood, accepted, and deeply connected at home.

When that connection is strong, it becomes a grounding force. It helps your teen feel secure in who they are, believe in their worth, and bounce back from life's inevitable stumbles. And it doesn't take grand gestures. Often, it starts with small, everyday moments—listening without rushing, showing up without fixing, and choosing words that build up rather than break down.

In this chapter, we'll explore what it means to truly connect with your teenager. We'll look at how your daily interactions, no matter how brief, can become the foundation for trust, self-worth, and emotional resilience.

Nurturing Connection through the Power of Presence

Recall a moment when you engaged in a heartfelt conversation with a friend. Here, you weren't just hearing words but truly listening, understanding emotions, and connecting with experiences. This is the essence of active listening, a powerful tool in building a strong relationship with your teen.

Active Listening

Active listening involves

- Paying full attention: Set aside distractions, focus on what your teen is saying.

- Acknowledging feelings: Validate their experiences without judgment.

- Reflecting back: Confirm understanding, like saying, "So you're feeling overwhelmed with the project because you're not sure where to start."

- Asking open-ended questions: Encourage expression, like "How did that make you feel?" or "What do you think you could do in this situation?"

By practicing active listening, you communicate to your teen that their feelings matter, creating a safe space for open, honest communication, and building trust and respect.

Non-Judgmental Attitude

A non-judgmental attitude is an open door, inviting your teen to express themselves without fear of criticism. This involves:

- Respecting their feelings: Even if you don't fully understand or agree.

- Avoiding criticism: Instead of saying, "You're being dramatic," say, "I can see that this is really upsetting you."

- Accepting your teen: Respecting their individuality, interests, and unique perspective.

By adopting a non-judgmental attitude, you reinforce that your love and acceptance are unconditional, fostering a sense of security and belonging, and strengthening your connection.

Consistent Availability

Tips for consistent availability

- Make time for quality interactions: Share meals, hobbies, or casual chats.

- Emotional availability: Be ready to listen and provide comfort, especially during challenges.

- Express openness: Let your teen know they can talk to you about anything, anytime.

Consistent availability shows your teen that you're a reliable, trustworthy source of support. This fosters a sense of security, boosts confidence, and strengthens your bond, creating a foundation for a thriving parent-teen relationship.

Cultivating Connection in Everyday Moments with Quality Time

Shared Hobbies

Immerse yourself and your teen in a shared hobby – whether it's gardening, building model airplanes, or playing chess. Beyond the activity itself, these moments are about connection, understanding, and joy. Shared hobbies create a relaxed, pressure-free environment for interaction, allowing conversations to flow naturally. You get to see your teen in a different light, appreciate their skills and passions, and express your pride and admiration.

Regular Family Meals

Sharing a meal is a powerful tool for connection. It offers a consistent platform for communication, providing an opportunity to catch up on each other's days, discuss topics of interest, and share thoughts and feelings. So, gather your family around the dinner table, surrounded by the aroma of a home-cooked meal and the hum of conversation.

Weekend Outings

Consider weekend outings as adventures, an escape from usual routines. Whether it's a hike in the local park, a movie night, or a museum visit, these outings provide a change of scenery that can refresh and rejuvenate your relationship with your teen.

Parenting Styles

As we said, no two children are alike, and a one-size-fits-all parenting style doesn't apply. As parents, we must be flexible, adapting our approach to our teenager's unique needs, personality, and the situation. Let's explore three common parenting styles and their influence on our connection with teens.

Authoritative Style

Think of this as the "sweet spot" in parenting. Authoritative parents set clear expectations and boundaries, but they also listen. They encourage their teens to make choices and learn from them, within a safe structure.

It's not about micromanaging every decision but about being available with guidance, support, and firm-but-fair consequences when needed. Teens raised this way often feel respected, heard, and empowered, which can make all the difference during these emotionally complex years.

Permissive Style

It's natural to want to be close to your teen—to be someone they confide in, laugh with, and feel safe around. Permissive parents often lean into this role, offering warmth and openness, but sometimes at the cost of structure.

While it's beautiful to be a source of emotional safety, teens still need boundaries to feel secure. The key is balance: be a trusted friend *and* a steady guide. Show unconditional love, but don't shy away from saying no or stepping in when needed. Structure isn't the opposite of love—it's an expression of it.

Authoritarian Style

This style is more traditional: think clear rules, little negotiation, and a strong focus on discipline. While it might keep things orderly on the surface, it can sometimes create distance between you and your teen.

If you've leaned toward this approach, consider softening the edges. Invite your teen into conversations, ask for their input, and explain the "why" behind your expectations. Discipline doesn't have to mean control – it can be a way to teach, to guide, and to build mutual respect. Teens respond far better when they feel seen and included, not just directed.

Building and Sustaining Trust

Creating a strong foundation of trust with your teen doesn't happen overnight. It's something that builds slowly through your words, your actions, and how you show up when it matters.

Let's explore what it looks like to nurture this kind of trust in practical, heartfelt ways:

Honesty and Transparency

Being honest with your teen doesn't mean telling them every detail of your adult world, but it *does* mean being real with them. If you're worried about their grades, for instance, it's more effective to share that concern calmly than to come down hard with criticism.

It also means owning your mistakes. Saying something as simple as, *"I was wrong, and I'm sorry,"* can go a long way in showing them that honesty is all about authenticity. Let them know what your expectations are and why. When rules and consequences are clear from the beginning, there's less room for misunderstandings.

Teens may not always *like* the boundaries, but when they see fairness and transparency behind them, they're more likely to trust your leadership.

<u>Reliability</u>

Trust is built in those everyday moments—being where you said you'd be, following through on promises, and being emotionally present. If you told your teen you'd be at their soccer game, be there. If you said you'd talk later, follow through. These may seem like small things, but to your teen, they speak volumes.

Being consistent with rules is another form of reliability. If curfew changes daily or consequences vary based on your mood, it creates confusion and erodes trust. But when your teen knows what to expect—and sees that you stick to your word—they begin to understand that your guidance is steady and dependable.

Respect for Privacy

As your teen grows, their need for privacy grows too. And while that might feel scary at times, respecting their space is one of the clearest ways to say, "I trust you." That said, respecting privacy doesn't mean turning a blind eye when you sense something's off. If you're concerned—whether it's about a sudden mood change, new friends, or risky behavior—have an open, honest conversation.

Instead of snooping, say, *"Hey, I've noticed you seem withdrawn lately. I'm not here to invade your space, but I care deeply about what's going on. Can we talk about it?"* That kind of approach preserves dignity while keeping the door to connection open.

How to Respect Privacy While Staying Involved

- **Knock Before Entering**

A simple knock signals respect for their personal space. It shows that their room isn't just a place in the house—it's *their* space, and you honor that.

- **Refrain from Intrusive Actions**

Reading journals or checking phones without consent chips away at the trust you're working so hard to build. If you're tempted, pause and ask yourself: *Is this about curiosity or concern?* If it's concern, have a direct conversation instead.

- **Encourage Independence**

Let them make decisions, even the small ones. Buying their clothes, managing their schedule, or planning outings teaches responsibility. These choices build confidence, which feeds back into trust.

- **Talk About Safety with Openness**

When you're genuinely worried, don't hide it. Share your feelings with honesty: *"I trust you, but I'm worried about some things I'm noticing. Can we talk about it together?"* Teens may not open up right away, but your steady presence makes it easier for them to come to you when they're ready.

- **Set Boundaries Together**

Boundaries work best when they're created *with* your teen, not just imposed. Sit down and talk about curfews, online rules, or social media use. When your teen feels involved in the process, they're more likely to respect the rules.

- ## Model Responsible Decision-Making

Your stories matter. Share what helped you make good choices, or what happened when you didn't. Show them that mistakes are part of life, and it's how we learn and grow that really counts.

Trust isn't just built during the big conversations—it grows every day as you remain consistent, respectful, and honest. It's reinforced every time you listen without judgment, hold a boundary with love, or step back and let them try (and maybe fail) on their own.

Chapter 12

Ready for Takeoff

Equipping Teens for the Real World

"For the longest, I was slightly naive when it came to the real world. There were a lot of fears I was afraid to conquer that were just holding me back from standing up for myself or taking chances." — Christina Milian

There comes a point when you look at your teen and think, *They're getting closer.* Closer to leaving the nest, to real-life responsibilities, and maybe, if you're honest, closer to a world that isn't always kind or predictable.

That moment comes with some form of pride and panic: *Have I prepared them enough? Do they know how to speak up for themselves? Will they know how to handle setbacks, or bills, or tough conversations?*

Christina Milian's quote above captures this perfectly. Many young people head out into the world a little wide-eyed, hopeful, yes, but also unsure. They might hesitate to speak up, afraid to make mistakes, or hold back from opportunities simply because they don't feel ready. But that's where we come in.

Helping our teens prepare for adulthood isn't about handing them a checklist of "how to be grown." It's about giving them the space and support to *become*. It's helping them practice decision-making while the stakes are still manageable. It's encouraging them to take chances, fall a bit, and get back up with stronger legs.

In this chapter, we're talking about the *real-world stuff*. Not just resumes or laundry (though yes, that too), but the internal skills—confidence, responsibility, resilience, assertiveness—that shape how they'll move through life. We'll talk about how to build those qualities without overwhelming them, how to create opportunities for growth right at home, and how to gently let go while still being their safety net.

It's okay if they're a little naïve at first. That's part of it. What matters most is that they leave with a sense of self-worth, the courage to take risks, and the knowledge that they are *capable.*

So, let's get started:

Nurturing Independence for the Real World

Financial Literacy

Remember the thrill of your first paycheck? It marked a step into independence, accompanied by newfound responsibilities. Financial literacy is a vital life skill that empowers teens for the real world.

- Mastering the Basics: Introduce teens to earning, spending, saving, and investing. Discuss budgeting, distinguishing needs from wants, and making informed spending choices. Familiarize them with various payment methods, from cash to digital wallets. Explain concepts like interest, loans, and the significance of emergency savings.

- Hands-On Experience: Make financial literacy practical. Involve teens in family budget planning or grocery shopping. Facilitate opening a bank account, encouraging them to save part of their allowance or job earnings. The goal is to integrate financial knowledge into daily life, building confidence for a secure financial future.

Basic Cooking Skills

- Starting Simple: Initiate with easy recipes like sandwiches or scrambled eggs. Progress to more complex dishes. Teach nutrition principles, reading food labels, and the importance of a balanced diet. Encourage exploration of various cuisines, flavor experimentation, and even recipe creation.

- Family Culinary Adventures: Transform cooking into a family affair. Initiate challenges like "cook with what you have" or designate a "make your own dinner" night. The objective isn't culinary expertise but instilling skills for preparing simple, nutritious meals independently.

Career Guidance

Career Interest Inventories

Navigational Tools

Think of career interest inventories as a guide, not something final. They're tools to help your teen reflect on what they enjoy, where their strengths lie, and how they might align with different fields.

These online assessments often ask questions like, *Do you prefer working alone or with others? Do you enjoy solving problems, helping people, and building things?* Based on their answers, the inventory suggests a list of potential career matches.

It's important to remind your teen: these results aren't set in stone. They're just opening the door to options they might not have considered.

Job Shadowing Opportunities

A Day in Their Shoes

Help your teen discover job shadowing chances in their areas of interest, whether with a veterinarian, software engineer, journalist, or chef.

Encourage them to ask questions, take notes, and reflect on the experience. *Did they find joy in the tasks? Did the work environment resonate with them? Could they envision themselves in a similar role?*

Job shadowing provides firsthand insights into the daily facets of a career, allowing teens to comprehend the specifics and assess alignment with their interests, skills, and aspirations.

College and Career Fairs

Strategic Engagement

College and career fairs might seem like just another event on the school calendar, but they're actually golden opportunities for teens to explore what's out there and start shaping their future with confidence.

To help your teen get the most out of these events, encourage a little prep beforehand. They can look up which schools, training programs, or companies will be there and do some quick research on the ones that catch their eye. This helps them show up with purpose—and some great questions in their back pocket. For instance, they can ask about course details, campus culture, and internship opportunities.

Navigating the Transition to Adulthood

Gradual Release of Responsibility

- Early Guidance: In the initial phases of adolescence, parents and educators serve as active guides, similar to driving instructors. Here, you provide crucial direction, set boundaries, and offer structure to your teen.

- Empowerment Through Release: As they grow older, it's important to slowly step back and let them take the wheel. Start by including them in decision-making, things like planning family outings or weighing in on big life choices, like future studies or career paths. Let them manage their time, take on new responsibilities, and even make mistakes. These are the moments where confidence takes root.

This shift doesn't happen overnight, though; it's a gradual, thoughtful process. It's about finding that balance between supporting them and trusting them to stand on their own.

Open Dialogues on Adulthood Realities

- Transparent Conversations: Keep the lines of communication open. Talk about what adulthood really looks like, not just the freedom, but also the responsibilities that come with it. Be honest, but also reassuring. Let them know you're there as a guide, not a judge.

- Informative Discussions: Keep in mind that these conversations are not about imposing expectations but rather enlightening them on the realities of adulthood. It's a preparatory dialogue, helping them comprehend the transformations they will undergo and equipping them for the journey ahead.

Celebrating Milestones

When your teen reaches a milestone, like landing their first job (even if just part-time), graduating, or getting that college acceptance, take a moment to celebrate. These aren't just boxes to check; they're markers of growth, of determination, of all the effort they've put in along the way.

These milestone celebrations serve as acknowledgments of their growth, expressions of gratitude for their efforts, and confidence boosters as they embrace the challenges and triumphs of adulthood.

CONCLUSION

Raising a teenager isn't something you prepare for with a checklist. It's something you live through, sometimes patiently, sometimes clumsily, often with a full heart and an exhausted spirit. And yet, here you are, showing up, learning, and adapting to make sure you do the best you can. That alone speaks volumes.

Over the past chapters, we've explored the adolescent brain from the inside out. We've looked at the emotional storms, the academic hurdles, the moments of defiance, and the victories. Through it all is a single truth: *your presence matters more than perceived perfection.*

Understanding how your teen's mind is changing helps you respond with more clarity and less frustration. Recognizing their emotional needs builds the kind of trust that outlasts tantrums and tempers. And supporting their academic journey—not with pressure, but with encouragement—can help them fall in love with learning, not just achievement.

I say this not as an expert in a white coat, but as a mother who's walked this path with two sons. I've seen firsthand how easy it is to feel overwhelmed, to question if you're doing enough–or too much. There were days when I felt like I was losing them to mood swings or silence. But slowly, through listening without fixing, guiding without forcing, and loving without condition, we became a team.

If there's one thing I've learned, it's this: teenagers don't need perfect parents. They need present ones. They need people willing to learn beside them, cry with them, laugh with them, and sometimes, just sit in the same room without saying a word.

So let this be your gentle reminder: every rough patch is an opportunity for growth. Every argument holds the potential for reconnection. And every time you choose to stay soft, even when everything feels hard, you are building the foundation to a solid relationship with your teen.

As we close this book, I leave you with this:

Be the lighthouse, not the lifeboat. You don't need to rescue them from every storm, but you do need to shine, steady and sure, so they always know how to find their way home.

Offer them roots, so they feel safe. Wings, so they feel free. And love, so they never doubt their worth.

Let them make mistakes. Let them fall and then be there when they rise. That rising, however slow, however messy, is what this whole journey is about.

With all my heart,

From one parent to another—

You've got this.

Book Thoughts & Opinions

D ear Readers,

I am writing to express my deepest gratitude for your support in reading my book. Your time and engagement mean the world to me. If you've enjoyed the journey through these pages, please consider leaving a review. Your words can guide and inspire other parents and educators, helping them discover the book and decide if it's the right fit for them.

Reviews are the lifeblood of independent authors, and your honest feedback can make a significant impact. Thank you for being a part of my literary journey, and I look forward to hearing from you.

To leave a review, go to your Order History, find the book under your purchases, and click "Write a Product

Review." If you're in the US, you can also scan the QR code below for quick access.

With gratitude,

Joyce T.

🎁 BONUS GIFT

As a gesture of gratitude, I'm delighted to offer you a complimentary copy of the e-book Bundled 2-in-1, aimed at enhancing your understanding of your child. This resource provides a comprehensive exploration of child development, spanning from embryo to teen.

Adolescent Brain 101 + Simplifying Child Development 2-in-1 Bundle

A Stage-by-Stage Guide to Nurturing a Healthy Child's Mind from Embryo to Teen

Scan the QR code to download with Access Code: mind

www.JoyceTbooks.com

References

1. American Psychological Association. (n.d.). The adolescent brain: Beyond raging hormones. Harvard Health Publishing. Retrieved from https://www.health.harvard.edu/mind-and-mood/the-adolescent-brain-beyond-raging-hormones

2. Bureau of Labor Statistics. (2015). Career planning for high schoolers. Retrieved from https://www.bls.gov/careeroutlook/2015/article/pdf/career-planning-for-high-schoolers.pdf

3. Center for Parenting Education. (n.d.). The skill of listening. Retrieved from https://centerforparentingeducation.org/library-of-articles/healthy-communication/the-skill-of-listening/

4. Cho, S., & Hall, J. R. (2016). Pubertal

development, emotion regulatory styles, and the... National Center for Biotechnology Information. Retrieved from https://www.ncbi.nlm.nih.gov/pmc/articles/PMC5061504/#:~:text=In%20this%20sense%2C%20adolescents%20with,diminish%20emotional%20clarity%20over%20time.

5. Choosing Therapy. (n.d.). Does my teen need counseling? 15 signs to know. Retrieved from https://www.choosingtherapy.com/does-my-teen-need-counseling/

6. Daniel Wong. (2022, June 14). How to communicate with teenagers (11 actionable tips). Retrieved from https://www.daniel-wong.com/2022/06/14/communicating-with-teens/

7. Empowering Parents. (n.d.). Hope for parents of defiant teens: 6 ways to parent more effectively. Retrieved from https://www.empoweringparents.com/article/hope-for-parents-of-defiant-teens-6-ways-to-parent-more-effectively/

8. Focus on the Family. (n.d.). Independence or rebellion? Retrieved

from https://www.focusonthefamily.com/parenting/independence-or-rebellion/

9. Good Therapy. (n.d.). Punishments vs. consequences: Teach your teen the difference. Retrieved from https://www.goodtherapy.org/blog/punishments-vs-consequences-teach-your-teen-the-difference-0427155/

10. Gottman Institute. (n.d.). Building trust with teenagers. Retrieved from https://www.gottman.com/blog/building-trust-with-teenagers/

11. Greater Good Science Center. (n.d.). How the teen brain transforms relationships. Retrieved from https://greatergood.berkeley.edu/article/item/how_the_teen_brain_transforms_relationships

12. Harvard Health Publishing. (n.d.). The adolescent brain: Beyond raging hormones. Harvard Health Publishing. Retrieved from https://www.health.harvard.edu/mind-and-mood/the-adolescent-brain-beyond-raging-hormones

13. Harvard Medical School. (n.d.). Screen time and the brain. Retrieved from https://hms.harvard.edu/news/screen-time-brain

14. Lessonbee. (n.d.). How social media can affect teenage self-esteem. Retrieved from https://lessonbee.com/blog/how-social-media-can-affect-teenage-self-esteem

15. LinkedIn. (n.d.). Digital detox and mental well-being: Examining the benefits... Retrieved f   r   o   m https://www.linkedin.com/pulse/digital-detox-mental-well-being-examining-benefits-unplugging-teenagers?trk=news-guest_share-article#:~:text=In%20conclusion%2C%20a%20digital%20detox,and%20promote%20healthier%20sleep%20patterns.

16. Mayo Clinic. (n.d.). Teen depression - Symptoms and causes. Retrieved from https://www.mayoclinic.org/diseases-conditions/teen-depression/symptoms-causes/syc-20350985

17. Michigan Department of Education. (2013, June 21). Adolescents: Discipline with the brain

in mind. Retrieved from https://www.michigan.gov/-/media/Project/Websites/mde/2013/11/01/Tips_for_Effective_Discipline_6-21-13.pdf?rev=50e829e1b2254298939606c0a017c11f

18. Middle Earth. (2014, April 14). 5 ways parents can teach assertiveness to teens. Retrieved from https://middleearthnj.org/2014/04/14/5-ways-parents-can-teach-assertiveness-to-teens/

19. National Academies. (n.d.). Open Case Studies: Mental Health of American Youth. Retrieved from https://www.opencasestudies.org/ocs-bp-youth-mental-health/

20. National Center for Biotechnology Information. (n.d.). Adolescent risk-taking, impulsivity, and brain development. Retrieved from https://www.ncbi.nlm.nih.gov/pmc/articles/PMC3445337/

21. National Center for Biotechnology Information. (n.d.). Later school start time: The impact of sleep on academic... Retrieved from https://www.ncbi.nlm.nih.gov/pmc/articles/PMC7177233/

22. National Center for Biotechnology Information. (n.d.). Prevalence and risk factors of cyberbullying and its... Retrieved from https://www.ncbi.nlm.nih.gov/pmc/articles/PMC9860135/

23. National Center for Biotechnology Information. (n.d.). Stress and the developing adolescent brain - PMC. Retrieved from https://www.ncbi.nlm.nih.gov/pmc/articles/PMC3601560/

24. National Center for Biotechnology Information. (n.d.). The emerging neuroscience of intrinsic motivation - PMC. Retrieved from https://www.ncbi.nlm.nih.gov/pmc/arti cles/PMC5364176/

25. National Center for Biotechnology Information. (n.d.). The influence of academic pressure on adolescents... Retrieved from https://www.ncbi.nlm.nih.gov/pmc/articles/PMC9534181/

26. National Center for Biotechnology Information. (n.d.). Types of parenting styles and effects on children. Retrieved from https://www.ncbi.nlm.nih.gov/books/NBK568743/

27. National University. (2022, January 20). Mindset and academic suc-

cess: What's the connection? Retrieved from https://www.national.edu/2022/01/20/how-mindset-can-help-academic-success/

28. Parent & Teen. (n.d.). Building resilience in teens: The 7 Cs. Retrieved from https://parentandteen.com/building-resilience-in-teens/

29. Positive Psychology. (n.d.). 16 delayed gratification exercises, worksheets & activities. Retrieved from https://positivepsychology.com/delayed-gratification-exercises-worksheets/

30. Positive Psychology. (n.d.). Promoting self-regulation in adolescents and young adults. Retrieved from https://fpg.unc.edu/sites/fpg.unc.edu/files/resources/reports-and-policy-briefs/Promoting%20Self-Regulation%20in%20Adolescents%20and%20Young%20Adults.pdf

31. RBC Wealth Management. (n.d.). Why financial literacy is an important life skill for youths. Retrieved from https://www.rbcwealthmanagement.com/en-ca/insights/why-financial-literacy-is-an-important-life-skill-for-youths

32. SheKnows. (n.d.). 24 essential cooking & baking skills your teen should... Retrieved from https://www.sheknows.com/food-and-re cipes/articles/1140231/cooking-skills-for-teens/

33. UNC Frank Porter Graham Child Development Institute. (n.d.). Effects of mindfulness-based intervention on adolescents. Retrieved from https://www.ncbi.nlm.nih.gov/p mc/articles/PMC8701759/

34. UNC Frank Porter Graham Child Development Institute. (n.d.). Promoting self-regulation in adolescents and young adults. Retrieved from https://fpg.unc.edu/sites/fpg.unc.edu/files/res ources/reports-and-policy-briefs/Promoting%2 0Self-Regulation%20in%20Adolescents%20and %20Young%20Adults.pdf

35. UNICEF Innocenti Research Centre. (n.d.). The Adolescent Brain: A second window of opportunity. Retrieved from https://www.unicef-irc.org/publications/pdf/a dolescent_brain_a_second_window_of_oppor tunity_a_compendium.pdf

36. University of Nebraska-Lincoln Extension. (n.d.). Friendships, peer influence, and peer pressure during... Retrieved from https://extensionpublications.unl.edu/assets/html/g1751/build/g1751.htm

37. Verywell Family. (n.d.). 8 essential strategies for raising a confident teen. Retrieved from https://www.verywellfamily.com/essential-strategies-for-raising-a-confident-teen-2611002